TERRARIA
& BOTTLE GARDENS

TERRARIA
& BOTTLE GARDENS

William Davidson

WARD LOCK LIMITED · LONDON

Acknowledgements

The publishers gratefully acknowledge the following agencies and photographers for granting permission to reproduce the following colour photographs: Harry Smith Horticultural Photographic Collection (front cover, pp. 6, 15, 18, 58, 75 and 78); Pat Brindley (pp. 14 and 56); Hyware Ltd (p. 10); Boys Syndication (p. 19 (upper)); John Glover (p. 27 (lower)); Photos Horticultural Picture Library (pp. 30, 39 and 47); and Peter McHoy (pp. 66 and 67).

All the line drawings are by Nils Solberg.

House editor Denis Ingram

Text filmset in Bembo
by Hourds Typographica, Stafford

Printed and bound in Portugal
by Resopal

British Library Cataloguing in Publication Data

Davidson, William
Terraria and bottle gardens.
1. Terrariums. Making
2. Bottles. Gardening
I. Title II. Series
635.9'824

ISBN 0-7063-6755-3

CONTENTS

Although, with the advent of the terrarium, the bottle garden has lost much of its appeal, it nevertheless makes an attractive room feature when planted with marantas, peperomias, selaginellas, trailing ficus and the like.

INTRODUCTION

BEGINNINGS

One could well be excused for thinking that the terrarium is quite a recent arrival on the plant scene, but the original concept goes back well over a century, to the distant days when it was fashionable for plant collectors to trek into the wild in search of hitherto unknown plants. Conveying seeds, bulbs and suchlike by the then slow means of transport was not too difficult, but getting live material from A to B was a challenge. Besides plants being sought for their decorative value, there were those being transported for commercial use. The rubber plantations in South-East Asia, for example, were stocked initially with plants from South America.

WARDIAN CASES

During this hectic time of plant introduction a gentleman named Nathaniel Ward had the idea of transporting live plant material in what were, in effect, miniature greenhouses. Doctor Ward's miniature greenhouses became known as Wardian cases, a name still current today, and were designed and constructed in the style of a traditional, ornate Victorian conservatory (Fig. i). New plants to stock the lavish conservatories of the wealthy were forever in demand at that time, and so plant hunters were sponsored to travel and seek out new plant material in the more exotic parts of the world.

Though Wardian cases were initially used for transporting plants across the oceans, they soon became decorative features in the grander homes of the day for housing smaller, more delicate plants that needed more warmth and humidity to succeed. Wardian cases later became less fashionable but some remained in use over the years and a few originals became museum pieces.

MODERN EQUIVALENTS

The Victorians were very fond of their plants, using them lavishly to decorate their homes and conservatories, despite the more primitive

Fig. 1 The original style of Wardian case, besides being decorative, offers ample head room for plants, so making planting easier and the end result more attractive. Genuine Wardian cases have become collectors' items.

means of heating, the presence of gas fumes and the generally poor light in their homes. But compared with the houseplant enthusiasts of today they were mere beginners. Since Tom Rochford coined the word 'house-plant' back in 1947, millions upon millions of these potted plants have been sold annually. The scale of the trade is quite unbelievable. You can now buy from all kinds of retailers the strangest exotic plants, some of tree-like proportions, others in the tiniest of pots.

With the plants and the small pots has come a renewed interest in Wardian cases, though they are now more likely to be called terraria or bottle gardens. The materials of which they are made and the quality of workmanship vary considerably, so it is worth shopping around to find what is most suitable in price and appearance. Plastic terraria will be cheapest, but like all things plastic they will not have the style or feel of something in glass and metal. The adventurous gardener might well feel that he or she would do better to buy a terrarium in kit form and assemble it at home.

With the advent of the terrarium the bottle garden has lost much of its appeal, as it is a much less satisfactory unit for displaying and caring for plants. In fact, the bottle itself has changed considerably. When bottles were first used to accommodate a collection of plants they were genuine carboys used for transporting acid, often in a protective metal frame and packed around with straw. If obtainable these carboys are excellent for growing plants in – and for being able to *see* the plants. The modern equivalent is mass-produced and a dirty green colour, so the plants have to live in a dark green bottle and are almost impossible to see unless you look into the mouth of the bottle. The greenness greatly reduces the amount of light reaching the plants within and in the poor light they become etiolated with abnormally small leaves and in time shrivel up and die. If you have a choice, do select a clear glass bottle – otherwise invest in a terrarium.

CARE AND DECORATION

When you consider buying a terrarium you will find that there are many kinds available at all sorts of prices. You often have to decide whether you are getting a stunning addition to your room furnishings or if you are getting something that will be of maximum benefit to your plants. The plants inside the container won't be in the least concerned about how splendid it is, but they will be much more impressed by the growing conditions they are provided with.

A plant wants its immediate environment to be light, warm, usually moist, and draught free. The sort of terrarium that best fits all these requirements is not a terrarium at all, but a tropical fish tank. A tank with clear glass and slender supporting pillars will ensure the plants enjoy the fullest amount of light – though plants in glass containers are best located out of *direct* sunlight. The tank offers a greater base area for planting and creating more interesting designs, and will be infinitely easier to plant.

If you want a container that is both aesthetically pleasing and ideal for your plants' well-being, you should buy one of the larger terraria with a large base area and good height. Many plants crowded into a small space are seldom effective as they cannot be appreciated individually, and the

Many modern terraria are made from plastic but nevertheless resemble glass. This attractive hexagonal design has a removable top and is available in standing or hanging versions.

congestion will inevitably lead to cultural problems. A plant cabinet should offer the plants good light, moist but not saturated conditions, and a temperature of around 15°C (59°F). There should also be no wild fluctuations in the water supply or the temperature.

Clean conditions are also vital, as pests and diseases will thrive in the agreeable conditions within a glass cabinet, whatever its type. It is also important to choose the right plants at the outset, and to use the best available materials when planting. The big bonus with terraria and the like is that, once planted, they require minimal care. In theory, you should simply sit back and enjoy them!

When shopping for plants for a terrarium one is normally offered green foliage plants, but there is much to be said for opting for some cacti, or a mixture of cacti and succulent plants. Cacti are much slower growing than green foliage plants and will require virtually no attention once they have been planted. Planting a terrarium with cacti is similar to settling in other plants, but greater care is needed when handling plants. Fish tanks that offer ease of planting are therefore more suitable than bottle gardens and other containers with restricted openings for introducing plants. Use a John Innes type compost with some additional grit for cacti to keep the mixture open and well aerated.

CHAPTER 2

CONTAINERS

In recent years the selection and quality of terraria has improved considerably, and there would appear to be a market for units of every size and price. Terraria are naturally sold in garden centres and in department stores, and it is not unusual to find them being soldered together on one of the stands at a flower show or similar event.

The least expensive units are made from durable plastic in traditional

Fig. 2 Modern plant propagators with high sides and a domed roof are ideal for planting as terrariums. Controlled temperature will also enable one to grow more delicate plants at comparatively little cost.

designs (Fig. 2) that visually have all the attributes of the more expensive glass models. Only when they are picked up does it become obvious that they are not the real thing. Many of the plastic units look as if they are made of smoked glass, which reduces the amount of light available to the plants within – a considerable disadvantage. But in other respects they can be planted and used in the same way as genuine glass and metal terraria.

One of the most popular of these plastic designs is shaped like a traditional free-standing Victorian pitched-roof conservatory. The roof of the unit is lifted off when planting to allow ample space for all the tasks that need to be done.

PLASTIC BOTTLES

The very cheapest of all containers that could be used as a terrarium is one of the clear plastic bottles that contain a variety of liquids for domestic use. If, with endless care and patience, a ship can be rigged up inside a bottle, then there is surely no reason why an imaginative plant person could not arrange a collection of plants within the confined space. But unlike the ship the plants will, hopefully, begin to grow, and you could be accused of cruelty to plants in such a confined space.

The more you think about the 'plants-in-a-bottle' idea the more imaginative you can become. If, for example, you have a plastic bottle why not cut the bottle along most of its length with a pair of sharp scissors so that part of the bottle can be hinged back to form a lid? You could then lay the bottle on its side, with a couple of wedges to stop it rolling, put in a little gravel, followed by some compost and a collection of tiny plants. Some fascinating tiny plants that come to mind are the living stones, the succulent Lithops, which, if planted with a few genuine stones can challenge visitors to point out which are stones and which are plants!

SWEET JARS

A discarded detergent bottle might be scoffed at as a container for slow-growing plants, but there is every chance that you could succeed with a plastic sweet jar from a confectioner's. Those with flat sides are better than the round ones if there is a choice but all these containers have quite large screw-top lids, which makes planting relatively easy. The lid can also be screwed into position after planting so that transpiration is reduced to a minimum and there is little need for watering. Having a reasonably wide mouth also makes maintenance easier. Clearly, a plastic

A sweet jar laid on its side (foreground) makes a good terrarium. Other objects can also be brought into service, such as large glasses and even plant-propagating cases.

Lantern-shaped purpose-made terraria are very popular and when tastefully planted make attractive centrepieces for tables.

detergent bottle or sweet jar would do little for the decoration of an elegant room but we are only suggesting them for reasons of economy and satisfying the needs of the plant person who is not concerned about elegance.

PURPOSE-MADE TERRARIA

If cash is no problem and elegance is required, making a choice of container can be difficult, as there is no shortage of models styled and constructed by true craftsmen. There are designs for every taste and every pocket, from the small single plant unit to free-standing cabinets costing a great deal of money by the time they have been planted, polished and put on sale.

Often a terrarium is so ornate and so grand that the plants inside it become almost incidental, when, to my mind, the position should be the reverse of this. The plants ought to be the main attraction. This implies that the container should be simple in design so that the plants within are set off to full advantage.

The disadvantage to the plants of most terraria is that the internal area is too restricted so that almost from the outset plants are touching the sides of the container and looking too cramped for comfort. In such restrictive, often airless conditions the plants will be much more vulnerable to fungal problems, particularly botrytis, which thrives on wet and rotting foliage and can completely destroy the plants in an overcrowded terrarium in a very short time.

FISH TANKS

Terraria are available that incorporate a tropical fish tank in their design, so that you not only have attractive plants to embellish your drawing room, but you can have highly coloured fishes to complete the picture. I should prefer tanks without the fish, tanks with clear glass sides and spacious enough to allow plants to develop, and to enable an imaginative plant person scope for attractive arrangements of plants. The advantages of using a fish tank (Fig. 3) rather than a conventional terrarium for plants are that the container is watertight, free of supporting struts so it offers good light, and it is very easy to put plants in position – and to attend to their needs, such as cleaning them, once they are planted and growing.

A fish tank can be fitted with a simple sheet glass lid, which can be slightly tilted to allow fresh air to enter, or removed altogether when planting or attending to the plants' needs. But you could opt for something more elaborate – perhaps a cover that incorporates a strip light that

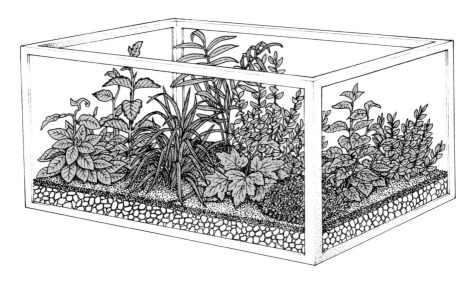

Fig. 3 This adapted fish tank shows clearly an attractive gravel layer beneath the potting compost – a feature that is both beneficial to the plants and aesthetically pleasing. Fish tanks also permit a more open style of planting.

encourages plant growth, such as Growlux. Plant growth will be much improved in such a unit and this will necessitate more frequent trimming of plants, or replanting them altogether. But the greatest benefit will be the generally improved appearance of the plants when the light is on. Almost any plant indoors, in a terrarium or not, will be much enhanced if it is stood under artificial light during the hours of darkness.

It is essential to ensure that the glass of these terraria is always clean, as blemishes show up like the proverbial sore thumb. The inside of the glass will also tend to be hazy as a result of condensation, and cleaning it can become a bore if it means removing the lid each time that cleaning is necessary. An alternative to the dishcloth for cleaning is a magnetic sponge (Fig. 4) which cleans the inside and outside of the glass at the same time. These are sold for cleaning house window panes that are difficult to reach, however long one's arms are.

If you have a fish tank custom-made to your requirements you could perhaps persuade the glazier to incorporate a mirror at the back of the unit rather than a sheet of clear glass. The mirror will be distracting at times, but this will be more than compensated for by the better appearance of the unit once it has been planted up. The mirror will reflect the

This modern octagonal terrarium has been planted with the colourful foliage begonia, *B. rex*, and with contrasting ferns.

Also very popular are purpose-made terraria in the shape of greenhouses. They make superb room features and are sufficiently large to enable one to create some imaginative planting schemes. This one includes a small palm.

Easier to plant than a bottle, but giving a similar effect, are glass bowls. These particular bowls have been planted with some choice gesneriads.

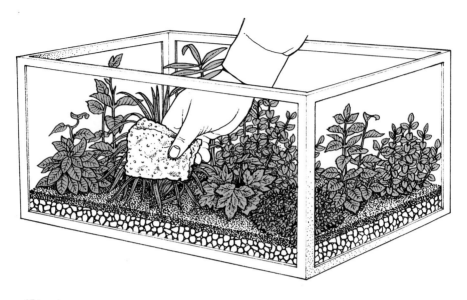

Fig. 4 Clean glass is essential if plants are to be fully appreciated. An absorbent sponge can be used to clean the glass and to wipe off excess condensation at the same time.

plants and make the container seem much deeper. If you are imaginative enough you can have a path leading through the plants to the mirror and seeming to go on much further.

Are you one of those enthusiastic plant lovers who is forever complaining that there is insufficient space for all the plants you would like to grow indoors? You probably need some ideas for growing the maximum number of plants. What about having several fish tanks tiered one on top of another from floor to ceiling so that you can have a collection of aerial gardens – all different, all individually lit and all looking marvellous. So much better than tired old wallpaper! Not practical, you may feel. Not a bit of it! Years ago when houseplants were still in their infancy an old acquaintance of mine (an engineer) built a range of aluminium shelves for his wife who was keen on indoor plants. Shelves is hardly the word, though, to describe these carefully engineered miniature greenhouses that were temperature-, humidity- and light-controlled and grew plants of the most splendid quality.

Space for plants was decidedly limited in their bungalow, so a spare bedroom was taken over and became the plant room, with these tiered miniature greenhouses occupying all of the surrounding wall space. The effect was quite wonderful with plants growing amazingly well in ideal conditions. The lady of the house was able to shut the door and tend or simply be with her plants without causing any inconvenience to anyone else. The units were all on castors which made it easy to wheel them outside when major work on the plants became necessary.

It would not be difficult to make a timber or metal framework in much the same way to support a collection of fish tank terraria. You see fish tanks used for their proper purpose in shops that sell fish and aquatics in general. All are lined against the walls for maximum effect and for the owner to house the largest possible range. It would seem perfectly feasible to a person who prefers plants to fish to present plants in terraria in precisely the same way. Such suggestions may have strayed from the original concept of the Wardian case, developed for transporting plants in good order while on long sea journeys, but it does indicate that there is far more scope to terraria than we sometimes realize.

COMPOST AND OTHER INGREDIENTS

You will see then that there is ample scope in respect of design, and wide variation in price when shopping around for terraria, but all need similar ingredients to ensure success. Having decided on your particular style of container you will have to turn to the houseplant department of your garden shop to acquire all the other bits and pieces needed to make your terrarium the success it ought to be. Have a word with the person in charge, who should be knowledgeable, and get them to provide some good quality soilless potting compost – something that feels good and is likely to be free draining, not a wet mess of sedge peat that is never likely to grow anything well. If there is a potting bench in the garden shop, it might be wise to suggest that you purchase a small bag of the compost that is in use there. It could be a deal better than the mixture in the sealed bag you take home . Bear in mind that if you do everything right but the potting compost is wrong, then your plants will have little chance of succeeding. You will need a small amount of charcoal to mix with the compost to prevent it becoming sour and covered in algae.

Buy enough washed pea gravel to give a good 2.5 cm (1 in) covering over the bottom of the chosen terrarium. The gravel must be washed clean under running water before it is introduced to the terrarium. You may fancy a few decorative ornaments to embellish the planting in the container, but do not overdo this. Having acquired the other essentials you only need the plants, of which a wide choice is described in the next chapter. It is important these are clean and free from pests and diseases. One whitefly can become a surprisingly large army when enjoying life in the confines of a warm, draught-free container.

Despite the manufacturer's claims for the wondrous qualities of his compost, you could find that once taken home and opened, it is not the sort of mixture in which your precious fittonias would wish to spend the rest of their life. The chosen compost might require a little 'doctoring' to grow plants successfully in a terrarium. After being stacked and palleted for transport, compost often becomes a wedge of dark, wet peat, much too damp and airless for plants in the confined space of a terrarium or bottle garden.

To overcome the 'wet and airless' problem you could empty the bag of compost into a large box and break up the chunks of peat with your hands. It could be worth compressing a fistful of the concoction at this stage to assess how much water it contains. The amount could surprise you. You could add dry peat to the mixture to dry it out a little, or add one part of perlite to two parts of compost. Work the perlite or peat into the compost with your hands and you will find you have a much more agreeable mixture – one that is well aerated, not too wet, and much more appealing to your fittonias or other plants.

CHAPTER 3

A TO Z OF TERRARIUM PLANTS

Plants for bottle gardens need to be small to get them into the bottle in the first place, and reasonably slow growing or easy to prune if they are not to become quickly overcrowded. It is a little different with terraria as they can range from small containers holding a couple of plants to very grand miniature conservatories capable of housing quite substantial plants.

The following plant selection provides for containers of all sizes. Although some plants will seem totally unsuited to your terrarium for baby plants, they will be fine for more elaborate models. Some of the chosen plants will be considered temporary when planted, flowering ones in particular, some will become overgrown, while others will need little attention over the years. The latter would seem ideal to many people, but you can get much pleasure from rearranging, replanting, and simply working with your plants to improve their appearance.

Achimenes

Temporary plants to contribute colour to larger terraria during spring and early summer, 'hot water plants' are deciduous and are started into growth in late winter following their winter rest. The foliage is not particularly attractive, but the flowers come in many bright shades. General care presents no problems. Store warm and dry during winter.

Acorus gramineus

A neat variegated rush that will form a pleasant contrast to other softer foliage in the terrarium. New plants are made by dividing older clumps at almost any time of the year. Being hardy outdoors, this plant is easy to manage, provided conditions do not become too hot and dry. It prefers moist conditions.

Aeschynanthus lobbianus

Belongs to the *Gesneriaceae* family, of which we seem to be seeing a wider selection stocked by the more adventurous plant retailers. Some are too large for an average terrarium, but others will be fine if plant growth can be allowed to trail out of an open window, where the bright and exotic cupped flowers can be seen to full advantage. Keep warm and shaded for best results.

Aglaonema
The *Araceae* family provides many exceptional houseplants, most of which are much too large and vigorous for confined areas. But most varieties of aglaonema are compact in habit and reasonably suitable for larger terraria. Growth generally forms a rosette at soil level and the plants are propagated by dividing these clumps. Keep warm, moist and shaded and begin with the smallest plants that you can find.

Alocasia
Another plant from the *Araceae* family and one that may cause a frown when suggested for a terrarium. But if you want to show off with your larger terrarium, the foliage of these fine plants is rarely matched. Some are much too large, but some, such as *A. lowii* with brilliant metallic blue-green foliage will be reasonably manageable. Humidity, warmth and shade are essential. Not a beginner's plant!

Anthurium
A. andreanum (painter's palette) is seldom offered for sale but is much too large anyway and not suited to confined spaces. But for larger terraria one could consider the freely available flamingo flower, *A. scherzerianum*, an unfortunate name but a plant with colourful red spathe flowers that does well in warm, humid, shaded conditions. Belonging to the *Araceae* family, it prefers peaty compost when potted or planted, and once established will respond to weak feeding. Some of the leaves may become large and ungainly, or plants may be bought in this condition, making them unsuitable for terraria, but removing a few leaves will do no real harm to the plant. It can be grown from seed, though this is a slow job.

Aphelandra
Once very popular *A. squarrosa* 'Louisae', the zebra plant, is now rarely seen – a pity as this was a fine plant, if a little large for bottles and glass cabinets. More suitable is the currently popular variety, *A. s.* 'Dania', which has silver and green leaves and the typical yellow bracts of the aphelandra. Ample water and feeding are most essential, also reasonable temperatures and filtered light.

Ardisia
At one time *Ardisia crispa*, the coralberry, was a very scarce plant, but it is now produced and grown much more satisfactorily in tropical regions

and exported in some quantity. Very slow growing, it has naturally glossy green foliage and attractive red berries on mature plants. Stems are stiff and upright, so older plants are only suitable for larger units.

Areca lutescens

This plant has the lovely alternative name of *Chrysalidocarpus lutescens*, or golden feather palm, and has bcome highly popular in recent years as shipments of seedling plants from tropical countries have increased. Mature plants would be unsuitable, but young plants with several seed-lings to a pot are generally available and would make fine plants for a terrarium or bottle garden until they outgrow their space. Avoid putting any sort of chemical on their leaves, keep them warm and moist and they will be little bother. Like all other healthy plants removed from a cabinet because they have become too large, the areca palm will form a majestic specimen plant if potted in peaty compost in a container whose size is proportional to its root development.

Azalea indica

In a cabinet of suitable size but not a bottle garden, an odd flowering plant can provide a fillip, even if it is only a temporary member of the collection. Azalea flowers come in many bright and pastel colours and give an exotic look to any plant collection. Do choose an azalea that is compact and in a reasonable sized pot. Many are grown in half-pots and have surprisingly little root system compared with the amount of top growth. Rather than plant it out, it is best to plunge the pot in the (large) terrarium's compost, so the plant can have individual attention, particu-larly as regards watering. Rather than pour water into the pot, it is best to remove the pot and plunge it in a bucket of rainwater and let all the air escape before removing it, letting it drain and then replacing it in the terrarium. This may seem a lot of bother, but the azalea is one of the finest flowering pot plants and worth a little extra attention.

Beaucarnia recurvata

An oddity if ever there was one and the sort of plant that you might be tempted to include with a collection of cacti in a terrarium, as it relishes dry conditions and develops a weird bulbous stem with stiffly recurving green leaves. It is also known as *Nolina recurvata* and, most appropriately, its common name is elephant foot. Slow to grow, these plants develop to tree proportions in time, though this is not something one would be too concerned about. Dry, light and airy conditions will suit them best, as they originate from the parched lands of southern Mexico, and they need feeding only on rare occasions when you happen to think about it.

Begonia

A large, varied and colourful family of plants grouped here under a single heading for ease of reference. There are cane types that grow very tall which would be totally unsuited to growing in a confined space, and flowering sorts that would quickly shed their blooms in a close atmosphere, so you have to choose some with care.

Best known of the foliage begonias are the *Begonia rex* types, which can vary in colour from bright silver to almost black. Even among the rex varieties are plants with leaves much too large for a terrarium, so care is needed here to select only plants with smaller leaves. Few will be labelled with varietal names in the plant shop, so there is little point in listing them. It's best to nose around in the shop for *B. rex* growing in larger pots just to see what size of leaf they develop. You could ask for advice, but in most establishments you could be confronted by a blank stare from an untrained assistant.

Of all the foliage houseplant introductions of recent years the one going under the name of *Begonia* 'Tiger' must surely be one of the most popular. With dull yellow spotting on a brownish green leaf this is a compact plant that will not be much bother to manage. If regularly potted on it could form a large mound of growth in time, but with roots restricted to a small body of compost it will remain more compact.

With longer leaf stalks and therefore more spreading, *Begonia* × 'Cleopatra' is a lovely plant of which good specimens will have foliage flushed with gold – especially attractive in good light. Several others of reasonably neat habit are worth considering for a terrarium or bottle garden.

Trailing begonias grown from tubers are reasonably common, but there are not many others that naturally trail. One of the exceptions is the lovely *B. sutherlandii*, which has the palest of pale green foliage and the most delightful trailing habit which shows off its clear orange flowers to perfection. In a terrarium that allows the plant to trail naturally out of an open 'window', it presents a very pleasing picture. Reasonably easy to care for and to propagate, it has one major drawback – mildew finds it particularly appetising and seems to eat the plant up in no time at all once the spores have become established. Mildew is a problem with many begonias and plants need constant inspection so that a fungicide may be applied at first sign of the disease.

Care of begonias during their more active season in spring and summer, when they must be kept moist, fed and in reasonable light, is not too difficult, but the winter months are more demanding. During this time they need to be kept very dry with no feeding whatsoever and at a minimum temperature of not less than 13°C (55°F). When planting in a

Gesneriads (plants in the *Gesneriaceae* family) are becoming more freely available and relish the warmth and humidity provided by a terrarium.

Best known of the foliage begonias are the *Begonia rex* types, which can vary in colour from bright silver to almost black. They are among the best foliage plants for terraria.

terrarium or bottle it is best to select small plants in small pots, as they are touchy about having their roots pulled about to facilitate planting. Take particular care that any plants put into a cabinet are free of mildew, as this fungus will thrive in the close conditions and get on to other plants too.

Beloperone guttata

Shrimp plant is the popular name of this plant, since the brownish orange coloured bracts are not unlike stranded shrimps. These are hungry plants that need good compost, and ample feeding once they have become established. Those bought from a plant shop will almost invariably be pot bound and in need of fresh compost immediately. Fresh compost and feeding will give you larger flowers and much brighter foliage. Pruning over-vigorous shoots will occasionally be necessary if plants are not to outgrow their welcome. Old flowering bracts should be removed as they fall, or before if possible, so that they do not lie among live foliage and set up rotting.

Bromeliads

Probably the best plants of all for terraria. Rather than split them under various genera, they are here described under the family umbrella of *Bromeliaceae*. All originate from tropical South America and with the exception of ananas, the pineapple, all are purely decorative. They can range in size from the minute *Tillandsia ionantha* to the majestic *Vriesia fenestralis*.

Most are exceptionally tough and durable plants that in their natural habitat grow among rocks and in the branches of trees. *Tillandsia usneoides*, Spanish moss, becomes a suffocating weed that needs no soil whatsoever as it festoons tree branches, even telegraph wires. In a warm, humid terrarium that offers reasonable height it is possible to grow Spanish moss by draping it over an old tree branch. Frequent spraying with water from a mister will help keep it alive.

Bromeliads are rosette-forming plants that may be self-coloured or multicoloured, as in *Neoregelia carolinae* 'Tricolor', many producing spectacular bracts from the centre of the rosette. The rosettes of many will change colour, becoming much brighter as the bracts or flowers appear. All rosettes naturally die after they have flowered. All is not lost though as a number of smaller rosettes will develop around the base of the old one before it completely disintegrates. These can be potted and grown on to form new individual plants.

Tillandsias and cryptanthus   These are the best plants for smaller terraria. The latter are known as earth stars, since the rosette of leaves is formed in the shape of a star, and the plants normally grow on the floor of the jungle rather than in trees. Small groups of plants such as *C. bromelioides*

'Tricolor' can be specially attractive in modest-sized terraria while the remarkable colouring and patterns in the leaves of *C. fosterianus* will be a knock-out in larger terraria. As few of these cryptanthus are freely available, it is often a matter of planting what can be found in your local shop. But they are worth seeking out, and in reasonable conditions are among the easiest of plants to care for.

Likewise, the tillandsias are almost indestructible, and are much more freely available, if priced rather excessively for the tiny plants they are. These are the little grey rosettes of foliage that almost every plant shop and department store sells as 'air plants' – some attached to tiny tree stumps or seashells, others in presentation boxes. These plants do particularly well in a terrarium because they are so durable and are slow growing to the point of being completely stationary!

Billbergia nutans   Queen's tears, or friendship plant is another much neglected toughie of the bromeliad tribe, with tall rosettes of grey foliage and remarkable pendulous bracts of largely bright pink and green colouring. A larger terrarium that will permit the bracts to hang from an opening will present a quite startling picture.

Vriesia splendens   Flaming sword is freely available and has banded rosettes of upright habit and flaming red, sword-like bracts that remain colourful for many weeks. A good, easy plant, especially if its bracts can be offered reasonable headroom to develop.

Neoregelia carolinae 'Tricolor'   The blushing bromeliad, as already mentioned, is one of the most spectacular of all plants, producing a flat rosette of colourful leaves becoming brilliant magenta-red in the centre as the flowers begin to form in the centre of the rosette. There are many other bromeliads of similar habit, but most of the these are only suitable for larger terraria.

Aechmeas   These are important members of the family and are very numerous. *Aechmea rhodocyanea* (also known as *A. fasciata*), the urn plant, is by far the most popular, with majestic downy grey rosettes and huge pink bracts with bright blue flowers. The overlapping leaves of this and many other bromeliads form a naturally watertight urn that must at all times be kept topped up with water. The water in the urns of older plants should be periodically changed, but there is no need for any feeding.

All these bromeliads are tough plants well worth seeking out.

Cacti and succulents

Another major group of plants of considerable interest to many owners of terraria and indoor plants in general, these are described together for easy reference (Figs. 5, 6 and 7). On page 82 there are several suggestions for a terrarium cactus garden.

Among the bromeliads, the air plants or atmospheric tillandsias are particularly suitable for terraria, due to their small size. Shown here is a typical example: *Tillandsia xerographica.*

Fig. 5 Cacti, in all their different shapes and sizes, are ideal for grouping together as sole occupants of glass units. Upright, rounded and spreading types should be chosen to provide maximum appeal and interest.

Fig. 6 Succulents such as echeverias and aloes will offer beautiful foliage of contrasting colour, as well as plants of interesting shape. Coloured stones added to the design will further enhance the overall appearance.

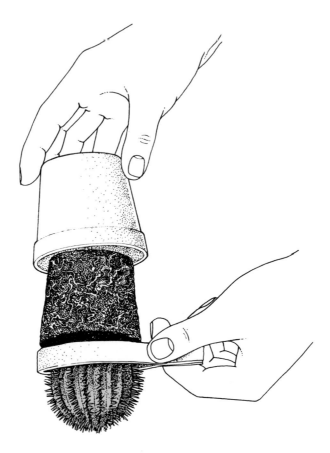

Fig. 7 Because of their natural protective spines, handling cacti can be troublesome. The use of a paper 'collar' when planting or potting will make the task easier.

Almost all of them are durable plants that require only moderate care to succeed. Their principal dislike is being too wet at the root, especially during the winter. Plants should be kept frost free over winter at a temperature of about 8°C (46°F), and from autumn through to spring will not require any water. This may seem harsh but this is how they would survive in their natural home.

Caladium
This is a bit ambitious perhaps, but there must come a time when a challenge is needed to prove that you are above average in plant care. Cala-

diums (angel's wings) belong to the *Araceae* family and have more delicate-looking foliage than most plants. But these leaves are deceptively durable and less likely to suffer damage than plants with more robust foliage. This is a spring and summer plant grown from a tuber and dying down in late summer, when it must be kept dry and warm until the end of the winter when the tuber can be put into fresh peaty compost, watered, kept very warm and started on its way for the ensuing season. It is by no means an easy plant, but it is a test of one's ability. A temporary terrarium occupant, it will need one of the larger cabinets as its leaves are fairly large and spreading. Those that spread too much can be neatly tied to a cane to tidy them up. The flowers are insignificant, but the leaves are in a class of their own, especially those of *C. candidum*, which are white with green venation and almost translucent. Other varieties come with red and lime-coloured leaves veined green.

Calathea makoyana

These members of the *Marantaceae* family, familiarly known as peacock plants, with large, highly decorative leaves, are only suited to larger terraria. Warm, humid, shaded conditions are essential, and it is important to check plants for the presence of red spider mites (generally indicated by dry-looking leaves with a pale brown discoloration on the reverse). These mites can be very troublesome on these plants. Feed in spring and summer.

Campanula

Two campanulas for a suspended terrarium or one attached at reasonably high vantage point against a wall in a conservatory – are *Campanula isophylla*, which is bright blue, and *C. isophylla* 'Alba', clear white. Both forms of the Italian bellflower are pendulous and free flowering for several weeks during the summer. Cool, light conditions will suit them and they should be cut back and kept on the dry side at the end of their natural season. New plants are not difficult to raise from cuttings a few centimetres long treated with rooting powder before being inserted in a peat and sand mixture.

Carex morrowii variegata

A hardy sedge sold as a houseplant in many plant shops, this is good for adding a different texture to a collection of foliage plants in terrarium or bottle garden. New plants can be raised from seeds if obtainable, though it is much easier to divide larger clumps into sections and pot these individually. Leave them to establish in their pots before introducing them to a terrarium.

Ceropegia woodii

A trailing plant of unusual habit, with strands of growth hanging down with grey-coloured heart-shaped succulent leaves that are likely to become an untidy tangle if not carefully handled – hence the common names 'hearts entangled' or 'rosary vine'. A comparatively easy plant to grow, it must be planted in a suspended or wall-mounted container, a terrarium with open 'windows' being ideal. Mature plants will develop peculiar bulbous growths on their stems which can be used to propagate fresh plants. If well cared for the strands of growth will hang down 2 m (6½ ft) or more. Tubular flowers may develop and set seeds.

Chamaedorea elegans

Equally well known by the name *Neanthe bella*, or parlour palm, this is perhaps the best palm for bottles and terraria as it is naturally dwarf and increases in height only when potted in relatively large pots after many years. When purchasing, seek pots containing more than one young plant then, if you need only small plants, divide the group to give you several plants. These plants are reasonably trouble free, but one of their pet hates is becoming excessively wet. They are considered almost indispensable for adding a little height to arrangements in smaller terraria and bottle gardens.

Chlorophytum capense

The ever-popular variegated grassy spider plant that will suffer many problems and still come through. Lovely in a suspended container when the parent plant produces its 'babies' on slender stalks that spray out in all directions. New plants are easily grown from these babies once they are well developed. Large, fleshy roots are produced in abundance on vigorous plants, so generous feeding is needed to keep the plant in good order. Browning of the leaf tips seems almost inevitable, and is due mainly to the plants becoming starved. Aphids on young leaves will cause distortion when these leaves mature, so keep a watchful eye for these pests. Plants will tend to become ragged with age, so need to be periodically replaced with fresh young stock.

Cocos weddelliana

Beautifully crisp miniature palms, now renamed *Syagrus weddelliana*, usually sold in long narrow pots with no drainage holes in their base. Only occasionally seen in plant shops but they are worth looking out for as they are a good alternative to the parlour palm, *Chamaedorea elegans*. Keep them moist, in good light (though not bright sun) and watch out for red spider mites on the undersides of their leaves.

There are many exciting gesneriads available these days, like episcias, aeschynanthus and small sinningias. All love the warmth and humidity found in fish tanks.

Codiaeum

More familiarly known as crotons, these come in many fine leaf colours – as bright as Joseph's coat, their common name. Most have leaves that are much too large to be confined in small spaces, but some, notably *C. pennick*, have narrow, mainly yellow foliage rather than the usual broad shape and will be fine in cabinets. A minimum temperature of around 15°C (59°F) is vital as plants will shed their leaves in dramatic fashion in winter if the temperature drops too low for any length of time. This is another plant favoured by red spider mites and because of the leaf colouring one on which the mites are difficult to detect. Regular precautionary spraying with recommended insecticide is one way of keeping them at bay.

Columnea

This is a truly neglected plant so far as houseplants go. *C. banksii* (and its variegated form) are occasionally available and is probably the most suitable for terraria, especially those suspended from a high vantage point. These plants are naturally pendulous with evergreen foliage attached to stiff, sometimes twisting stems, with superb orange flowers during the early months of the year. Others are much larger in habit, but are also inclined to be more difficult to care for. *C. banksii* and its forms would be ideal plants in an open-sided terrarium in a conservatory offering a little headroom, filtered light and reasonable temperature. Cuttings taken after flowering and placed in a heated propagator should root without difficulty.

Cordyline terminalis

This plant's brilliant red leaves are not to everyone's taste, but it is attractive if its colouring can be blended with neighbouring plants. Although short in growth this plant is of bold appearance and will need to be grown in a large cabinet. A temperature of around 15°C (59°F) will be necessary and careful watering to avoid compost becoming permanently saturated. Feed weekly while in active growth, but give none in winter when it also needs less water.

Crossandra

A neat glossy-leaved plant that needs to be kept warm and moist to thrive, *C. infundibuliformis* is better known as the firecracker plant. Flowers of the variety most often offered for sale – 'Mona Wallhead' – are orange red, attached to stiff upright stems and produced in spring and early summer. The leaves are reasonably attractive even when the plant is not in flower. New plants can be made from short cuttings taken at any time, but these need a high temperature to root. Water freely during spring and summer, but give much less, and no fertilizer, in winter.

Cuphea ignea

Commonly called the cigar plant, this is sometimes labelled *C. platycentra*. Though it is evergreen, fresh plants are usually grown from spring-sown seeds each year. New plants can also be raised from cuttings. The common name derives from what looks like cigar ash at the tips of the tubular flowers. A very easy plant to manage if given reasonable growing conditions.

Cycas revoluta

Said to be the oldest kind of plant in existence, this cycas, the sago palm, develops an attractive trunk as it ages, but ageing is a long process. Young plants are occasionally available but are invariably costly, so it is not everyone's plant. One of these would need a really special sort of cabinet in which the plant could be housed with very little else other than perhaps a few well chosen stones, a gnarled branch and a few pads of bun moss. It could then be put reverently on display rather like the crown jewels! A superb plant standing in solitary glory would certainly be more effective than the same plant crammed in among a motley collection of oddments.

Cyclamen persicum

A notoriously difficult plant for some people, but for those who provide cool, airy conditions and water only when necessary this is one of the finest of all our flowering pot plants. You won't get it into a bottle garden, but it can offer pleasing colour and coolness for a terrarium for almost the whole of the winter if you are prepared to replace plants that have passed their best. These are definitely temporary plants that should be left in their pots so they can have individual treatment and be easily replaced once they have faded. Plants that suddenly collapse for no apparent reason could be suffering from vine weevil grubs attacking their roots. These are difficult pests to eradicate, and once plants have collapsed they can only be consigned to the rubbish bin.

Dieffenbachia

Colourful members of the *Araceae* family, these are the 'dumb canes', of which some varieties, such as 'Tropic Snow', are much too large for terraria of any kind. But those with smaller leaves and less robust growth, such as *D. camilla*, can be housed in larger cabinets at least for the early part of their existence. The plant's sap is poisonous, so it is important to wear gloves when handling it, especially if the foliage is wet. Keep minimum temperature of around $15°$C ($59°$F) and reasonably moist compost at all times, giving rather less water in winter.

Dizygotheca elegantissima

A long name for this member of the family *Araliaceae*, though it may also be purchased by the less formidable name of *Aralia elegantissima*. Young plants have blackish green leaves that radiate from stiff upright stems, forming an attractive plant when in its juvenile stage. But as the years pass the foliage coarsens as leaves take on their adult form and the plant is much less attractive. But as this process takes many years the planter of terraria should not be concerned. As a young plant it is excellent for giving a little height to a terrarium or bottle garden. Plants are raised from seeds, not available outside the commercial world, and are generally sold in small pots ideal for planting in cabinets, fish tanks or whatever.

Dracaena marginata

There are many fine dracaenas offering superb decorative value among our houseplants, but very few, other than *D. marginata*, the Madagascar dragon tree, are suitable for our purpose. This one only fits while in its young stage. In time it will grow to a substantial height, its lower leaves will all have disappeared and the plant will have lost much of its attraction. The leaves are a dull shade of green with a dull red margin and the growth is perfectly upright. As with all these dracaenas, loss of the lower leaves is inevitable as plants increase in height.

Episcia

A much neglected group of plants that ought to be more popular with the commercial growers and the general public. *E. cupreata* (flame violet) has numerous forms, all with the most attractive leaves and small, brightly coloured flowers. Reputed to be a creeper (making it at home in a bottle or terrarium), it is also a very fine pendulous plant for a suspended terrarium with an open side for growth to escape from. Not easily acquired, but these are fine plants worth hunting for if you can provide the warm conditions that are essential for success.

Another of these neglected plants is *E. dianthiflora*, with the common name of snowflake plant or lace flowers on account of its white flowers which have frilled edges and certainly resemble snowflakes. A natural trailer with green leaves formed in a rosette and attached to stiff pendulous stems. Easy to propagate, easy to grow and lovely when in flower – not so difficult to obtain either.

The polka dot plant, *Hypoestes sanguinolenta*, seems to be in just about every terrarium and bottle garden, as well it might, since it is one of the most attractive plants introduced for many years.

Euonymus

Versatile as hardy garden plants, these are also sold for indoor decoration and will be found among bottle garden plants in garden shops. Most have silver- or golden-variegated foliage. Easy to manage, they need good light and modest temperatures. Plants form neat mounds of growth and will need an occasional trim.

Exacum affine

A temporary terrarium plant that can be grown from seed or bought in flower to liven up the rather larger terrarium that may be looking a bit drab. The single flowers of the Arabian violet are blue with a yellow eye and often have a delightful fragrance. Keep moist and in reasonable light, and feed occasionally. Discard after flowering.

Fatshedera lizei

There are green and variegated forms of this man-made cross between a fatsia and a hedera. Naturally erect plants, they are available as 'tots' for smaller planting units, or as taller specimens where height is available. Good light, avoiding direct sun, and cool rather than warm conditions suit them best. Avoid overwet conditions and feed now and then.

Ferns

There are many to choose from, though many, such as the splendid nephrolepis, become much too large for all but giant terraria. Generally speaking, ferns need to be reasonably warm with a minimum temperature of 13°C (55°F), and shade from direct sunlight is essential. Moist rather than dry conditions are also to be preferred. If plants dry out excessively their foliage will shrivel alarmingly and the plant will die.

Ferns of every description are favourites for selling as 'tots' in plant shops and are generally available in a wide range. But few if any will be properly named and at the early stages of growth it is not easy to distinguish between them, so you could be unwittingly buying something that in time will become much too large for the available space. As mentioned before, you can seek information from the staff about the proper names for their small ferns, but it might be better to check the little plants against larger ones on the benches, to help you identify them.

Adiantum radianum

Commonly known as the maidenhair fern. There are numerous kinds all with the unmistakably delicate pale and dark green foliage used the world over for room decoration. Moist, warm and shaded conditions are essential. If the compost dries out, the foliage will shrivel with the possible loss of the entire plant. Where practical, it will benefit this and other ferns to mist over the foliage occasionally with a hand sprayer filled with water that is tepid, not cold.

Asplenium
The spleenworts develop into majestic plants in time, but in their early stages could usefully be included in containers of reasonable size. The bird's nest fern, *A. nidus*, has pale green glossy leaves, arranged like the feathers on a shuttlecock. Keep a watchful eye for scale insects.

Pellaea rotundifolia
A lovely plant for all but the smallest units, the button fern is a low-growing plant with dark rounded leaflets that are a perfect foil for more colourful foliage. An easy plant.

Pteris
There are several forms of brake fern suitable for a terrarium, some with bright coloured fronds, and mostly easy to please in good conditions. Some will become too tall, but snipping off the more robust fronds will keep them under control.

Ficus
The figs are an important family among our houseplants but most are far too large and vigorous to be considered for bottle gardens or terraria. Only one is suitable for our purpose and that is *F. pumila*, the creeping fig. Suitable is hardly the right word, as it is almost the perfect plant. It creeps over the compost and will in time creep along the moist internal glass, and can be trimmed to shape at any time if it becomes too invasive. Its leaves are pale green, oval shaped, and attached to stiff stems. Care is easy, provided conditions are moist, warm and light though not sunny.

Fittonia
In size and habit these are fine plants, but they are a touch temperamental and not really for beginners. The most difficult is the red-veined one that goes under the rather grand name of *F. verschaffeltii*, the painted net leaf. This one also develops somewhat larger leaves, so is not ideal for small units. Of less robust habit is the silvery leaved one with very fine darker venation that bears the name *F. argyroneura* or silver net leaf. The best for our purpose, however, is the smaller version of this which has the additional name *nana*, indicating that it is dwarf. Leaves of the latter are very attractive and the plant has a low, creeping habit, ideal for warm, shaded, moist situations.

Gardenia jasminoides
These can develop into substantial shrubs in time, but in their early stages can be exotic occupants of the larger cabinet. The glossy evergreen foliage is a perfect foil for the creamy white flowers that have the most wonderful fragrance of almost all plants – their scent is the main attraction. Keep moist, shaded and warm, avoiding very wet root conditions.

Glechoma
Glechoma hederacea, the so-called ground ivy, is much used as a slender trailing plant in hanging baskets outdoors, but it can also be very effective in a conservatory as a trailing plant in a suspended terrarium. Not a wildly attractive plant, but it will help add another dimension to arrangements of mixed plants. Very easy to manage.

Gynura sarmentosa
The purple nettle or velvet plant has brilliantly coloured foliage in full sun, but its flowers have the most abominable odour one could imagine, so are not to be recommended. This plant is really included here to put you off it, as it grows at a prodigious rate, and quickly fills an agreeably warm terrarium. Perhaps it would be tolerable grown as a trailer spilling out of the windows of a suspended unit. Very easy to care for. Remove its buds before they can open!

Haemanthus
An odd choice perhaps, but including a few unusual plants will add interest to the planting. Seldom offered for sale, the paintbrush plant, *H. albiflos*, is normally acquired from a friend. Wide, leathery leaves grow from a bulbous base and are not much in themselves, but plants improve enormously when the white brush flower appears in the centre of the plant. Very easy to manage.

Hedera
Lovely plants the ivies, many with small variegated leaves that are ideal for units in cooler rooms. They will climb, creep or trail and can be pruned to shape at any time. Very attractive in suspended units (Fig. 8), or those attached to a wall, as the trailing foliage can then be seen to full advantage. Red spider mites can be a problem, so avoid very dry conditions, and use a systemic insecticide when necessary.

Helxine
Commonly named 'mind your own business' or 'baby's tears'. *Helxine* (or *Soleirolia*) *soleirolii* might seem ideal at first sight, with its neat creep-

Fig. 8 Many terrarium designs have open 'windows' to allow the inclusion of hanging plants. Such units can look particularly effective when suspended from a ceiling or wall brackets.

ing foliage, either green, silver or golden in colour. But in damp conditions it can be extremely invasive, so be warned and keep it well under control. Any small piece will root at almost any time in damp compost.

Hoya

The prettiest of these is *Hoya bella*, the miniature wax plant, with pendulous clusters of jewel-like flowers, but caring for it can be a problem, and it really is too spreading for most terrarium units. Perhaps a misshapen, one-sided plant with leaves over one side of its container could be persuaded to look the part by allowing the foliage to push out of a unit window. The more vigorous *H. carnosa*, wax flower, is a plant with potential for a larger unit if its growth is kept under control by attaching it to some neat trellis, rather than allowing it to scramble everywhere. This species is easy to care for.

Hypocyrta nummularia
The compact clog plant has odd-shaped orange flowers and is a reasonably easy plant to manage. If given ample space in a large suspended container this plant will develop into a large clump in time, though it can be restrained by restricting its roots in a smaller container. Keep it in good light at a reasonable temperature (minimum 13°C (55°F)) and avoid wet conditions.

Hypoestes sanguinolenta
The polka dot plant with its gaudy bright pink spotted foliage seems to be in just about every terrarium and bottle garden, as well it might, since it is one of the most attractive plants introduced for many years. As they age these plants become much taller and lose their compact appearance, but they can be pruned before they become too tall to retain their shape. Reasonably easy to care for, they need good light to retain their attractive colouring. An essential plant sold in vast numbers.

Impatiens
Impatiens (busy lizzies) grown from seed tend to be too vigorous for our purpose, and could only be used as temporary plants if included in a terrarium. But the 'New Guinea Hybrids' grown more for their colourful foliage than for their flowers are a possibility for larger units. Choose plants with bright coloured foliage only – many are very green and much less interesting. Plenty of moisture and frequent feeding are essential for these plants. New plants can easily be raised from firm cuttings in warm conditions.

Iresine
An easy plant in several colourful varieties that deserves to be more popular. Grown almost entirely for its foliage, the species *Iresine herbstii* (beefsteak plant) is a brilliant crimson and useful for many purposes, not least for brightening up the interior of a larger cabinet that will allow room for reasonable growth. Plants can be pruned to shape at any time, and the trimmings will not be difficult to root in a peat and sand mixture.

Kalanchoë

As commercial flowering pot plants, *Kalanchoë blossfeldiana* (flaming Katy) varieties have become almost the most popular of all that are produced – available in four or five good colours they are very easy to manage if grown in good light. When they become too large for a terrarium they should be removed and potted in appropriate sized containers and the gap in the terrarium filled with a fresh, young plant. A very interesting kalanchoë for a terrarium is *K. pumila*, a plant with powdery grey foliage that is naturally pendulous. It will add interest to any collection. Getting hold of plants is not easy, but they are well worth seeking out.

Mikania

A reasonably easy plant with wine-red foliage and a naturally pendulous habit, *Mikania ternata* would only suit a suspended unit or one attached to a wall where its growth could be trained to hang from open windows. The clumps of growth become heavy and less attractive in time and will need to be thinned out and cut back. Easy plants.

Nertera depressa

The bead plant has foliage not unlike that of helxine, but there is added interest from masses of bright orange berries nestling among its leaves. Producing these on a commercial scale is a highly professional business and few nurserymen attempt to grow them. This is reflected in the high asking price. But these plants can be both colourful and extremely interesting as carpet plants in containers of reasonable size. Keep them in reasonable light and avoid getting them too wet.

Pellionia

Pellionia daveauana, the so-called trailing water-melon begonia from Burma and Vietnam is only occasionally offered for sale, yet is fine for terraria. Being of a naturally creeping habit they will soon cover the surface of the compost, and can be allowed to trail over the side of the container if you wish. These plants are grown for their colourful foliage and are easily propagated from cuttings.

Peperomia

These are generally neat plants, suited to terraria and bottle gardens, and there is almost always a good selection in a plant shop. *P. magnoliaefolia* (desert privet) with fleshy cream and green leaves is probably the most popular and a good plant for terraria and bottle gardens. Overwatering is the main cause of trouble in its cultivation, so needs to be watched.

Reasonable temperature and good light are also important. *P. caperata* (emerald ripple) with dark green crinkled leaves of rounded shape on compact plants has always been popular and retains its pleasant appearance for a long time.

Philodendron
Many magnificent plants here, but only one that is reasonably suitable for our purpose. This is *P. scandens*, the sweetheart plant, best for the larger units. With heart-shaped evergreen leaves it will climb or trail depending on what is required of it. For a terrarium it looks best trailing over the rim of the container. Leaves should be kept clean, and moist, warm and shaded conditions suit them best.

Pilea
The aluminium plant, *P. cadierei*, gets its common name from the naturally silver gloss on its foliage. Very easy plants to care for and to propagate from firm cuttings, they will adapt to a wide variety of conditions provided it is not too cold. Plants can be pruned to shape at any time, and do best in good light, modest warmth and moist but not overwet compost.

Piper
Piper ornatum is an ornamental pepper that will test the skills of every grower, however accomplished. Its deep green leaves have silver and pink markings which combine to form very unusual foliage colouring. Plants need warm, moist and lightly shaded conditions to thrive and are only suited to larger cabinets that afford the plant reasonable headroom. There are other kinds, all scarce, but this is the one that is most often seen.

Plectranthus
Another scarce plant in shops, but one that is extremely easy to propagate from cuttings at any time of the year, *P. oertendahlii* is better known as Swedish ivy. A few snippets from a friend is the usual way of acquiring it. Grown solely for their foliage and ease of growth, these plants will creep or trail, depending on the facilities offered them. Easy to care for and can be pruned at any time.

Pleomele
The exquisite *P. reflexa*, or song of India, also sold as *Dracaena reflexa*, is an incredible plant with rich yellow leaves on gently twisting stems that will reach a height of some 2 m ($6\frac{1}{2}$ ft) when grown in a pot. But this takes a long time and small plants are perfectly suitable for larger cabinets

There are many lovely green and golden forms of selaginellas – the perfect terrarium and bottle-garden plants. Conditions must be warm for the plants to prosper.

until they outgrow their allotted space. Buy the smallest good quality plants available and grow them in good light in a modest temperature and avoid overwet conditions.

Polyscias

A plant of very slow growth, fine for providing a little height in a moderate-sized cabinet. There are several varieties with *P. balfouriana* (dinner plate aralia) with pleasantly variegated foliage possibly the best. These plants are now much more freely available and resemble indoor bonsai on account of their woody stems and very slow rate of growth. Keep moist and in reasonable light for best results.

Primula

There are many of these, some of which are suitable and then only for temporary brighteners for terraria. All need moist, light and cool conditions to succeed. *Primula malacoides* (fairy primrose) in its many lovely colours is one of the best on account of its compact habit of growth. Remove flower stems as they die and dispose of the plant after flowering.

Saintpaulia

One of the best flowering plants to include in a cabinet as these African violets enjoy the draught-free situation and the generally more agreeable conditions that prevail in a well managed terrarium. Buy plants in small pots rather than large ones as this will make planting much easier. Larger pots will contain a larger root ball and many of the roots are bound to get broken if planting is done properly.

There has always been a wide range of colours in these plants' flowers, but there are now miniatures too and even trailing African violets, which adds greatly to their interest and also makes them much better plants for a terrarium. Some nurseries specialize in these plants and will be only too pleased to send details. Alternatively, they can be seen and purchased at various flower shows staged around the country.

For the confined space of smaller terraria there are even micro saint-paulias – the variety 'Pipsqueak' has a diameter of little more than 6 cm ($2\frac{1}{4}$ in). Both trailing and miniature types require the same care as the more conventional larger plants.

Where possible it is better to select plants for a terrarium with a single rosette of leaves from which flowers are sprouting, rather than clumpy plants with masses of leaves from which flowers are fighting to emerge. A congested plant will present more problems with rotting and general care. To reduce the risk of rotting and the presence of botrytis fungus it is essential to keep everything spotlessly clean. This will mean regular inspection of all flowering plants, especially saintpaulias, and removing all dead and dying leaves and flowers. To remove dead leaves and flowers hold the plant firmly in one hand and remove the entire leaf or flower with its entire stalk with the other. Any odd pieces left attached to the plant will rot and cause trouble later.

Keep water off leaves when watering, and always use tepid water rather than cold water straight from the tap. If plants become too large and spreading it will do no harm to remove some of the outer leaves, again making sure that the whole of the leaf stalk is detached. Don't expose plants to direct sunlight when they are growing in a glass container, and be sure to maintain an adequate temperature – around 18°C (64°F) is suggested as a minimum. These plants need some warmth to do well. In an enclosed container it is seldom necessary to clean the leaves, but if this is done use a soft brush gently to wipe the leaves, rather than rubbing them with a sponge.

Sansevieria
The much abused 'mother-in-law's tongue' is an almost indestructible plant if kept reasonably warm and very much on the dry side. Most are too large to include in cabinets of any kind but the rosette-forming *S. hahnii* and its variegated form are among the best plants for our purpose as they are neat and rarely outgrow their welcome. They are also as tough as old boots, giving little or no bother.

Saxifraga stolonifera
The 'Tricolor' form of 'mother of thousands' is the better plant if there is a choice but the conventional *S. stolonifera* will be much easier to grow and will be more liberal in producing the pendulous baby plants that are its prime attraction. Pendulous plants rightly suggests that a hanging or wall-mounted terrarium will be most suitable. Moderation is the order of the day – a modest temperature and amount of light and careful use of the watering can. New plants are started from mature 'babies'.

Selaginella
There are many lovely green and golden forms of these perfect terrarium and bottle garden plants. Feathery growth develops into neat mounds of greenery (or of a golden colour) but it must be warm and moist for the plants to prosper. Though often seen labelled as ferns they are in fact closer to mosses. They will not always be named in plant shops, so you would be wise to take some photographs with you if you wish to identify the plants.

Sonerila
Difficult, but interesting plants with unusual leaf colouring that in the most popular variety, *S. margaritacea*, are purple on the underside and white and green on the upper surface. This plant needs to be grown in good light but not in direct sunlight. It is also wise to keep water off its foliage. If possible, keep a minimum temperature of approximately 15°C (59°F).

Spathiphyllum

The variety 'Mauna Loa' has now almost completely superseded the original *S. wallisii* (peace lily or white sail), but the latter is smaller and more compact, so better suited for our purpose. Even so it would be necessary to reduce the size of larger clumps of leaves to make them more manageable in a terrarium. For a really splendid cabinet of good overall size and particularly height, you could think of planting just 'Mauna Loa' with perhaps a few wisps of ivy at the base and hanging from the open windows. Sensible folk would say this plant is far too large for terrarium planting, but she is such a beauty and totally without temperament, which can't be bad!

Stephanotis floribunda

Perhaps another insane suggestion, but there is not much that compares with the fragrance of this plant's flowers. In a conservatory you may well get away with the Madagascar jasmine spilling from your splendid cabinet to the considerable envy of everyone who casts an eye on it. Good light is important, as it will be to keep a watchful eye for mealy bugs. Water fairly freely in spring and summer but give much less in winter. Feed only when active, never in winter.

Streptocarpus

The older variety 'Constant Nymph' and the more modern hybrids of the Cape primrose are splendid plants but do have rather large leaves that really rule them out, but one of the nicest of plants, and a touch uncommon, is *S. saxorum*, the false African violet. Its leaves are small, green and succulent, forming a dense mass from which emerge the most enchanting blue streptocarpus flowers. These are sparse, varying in numbers with changing conditions, but are there for most of the year. Easily propagated from a piece of leaf, they add charm to almost any cabinet.

Stromanthe amabile

Belonging to the *Marantaceae* family and closely resembling marantas, these are pleasing plants for a mixed group on account of their decorative foliage and neat habit of growth. Like marantas they call for warm conditions with 15°C (59°F) as a minimum, and shaded moistness as opposed to a hot and dry atmosphere. Older clumps can be divided and planted individually to provide new plants.

Syngonium

Another member of the splendid *Araceae* family which has arrowhead shaped leaves in many shades of green, *S. podophyllum* is also known as the goosefoot plant. It would be essential to start with the smallest available plants and then remove them from the unit when they become overgrown. They can be potted individually to make room for replacement plants. Keep moist, shaded and warm.

Tolmiea

The pick-a-back plant carries its young on the older leaves. These can be detached when of manageable size to make new plants. The benefit of this plant is that it is perfectly hardy, so well adapted to a colder room or conservatory. Watch for the presence of red spider mites and select the smallest plants available when planting.

Tradescantia

One of the humbler members of the houseplant league, but there are some fine plants among the tradescantias that will provide ample reward if given reasonable care. Almost any piece of these will root with ease, with reduced success only in winter. Avoid planting bold clumps as all these 'trads' will grow a pace. Over-vigorous growth can be trimmed at any time and the pieces used to propagate new plants.

Tradescantia fluminensis (wandering Jew) types include 'Silver', with typical small silver leaves produced in great profusion. With similar leaves 'Golden' speaks for itself, and then there is 'Rosea', a delightful plant with foliage in lovely pale pink shades. An altogether bolder plant with larger leaves and more vigorous growth is 'Quicksilver', which would only be suitable for larger cabinets where growth could spill out of its open windows.

In the same family and very similar in habit is Zebrina pendula, the silvery inch plant or (again) wandering Jew, a splendid if common plant with superb silvery colouring on the upper surfaces of its leaves and rich burgundy on the reverse. All of these are naturally pendulous plants, so provide for them accordingly. Be careful to avoid wet and dark conditions.

Vinca

Finally we have a neat little flowering plant, Vinca rosea, recently renamed Catharanthus roseus, that can be used as a temporary spot of colour during the summer. Its single flowers in clear colours – pink, white, or white with a pink centre – are offset by very compact greyish green foliage. Keep these plants moist, cool and in good light for them to do well.

Having considered the sort of plants one might choose to plant in a container, it should be added that terraria and fish tanks not only make attractive features when filled with a selection of plants, but are almost perfect propagating cases. A wide assortment of cuttings can be rooted in them to provide material ready for the time when the terrarium or bottle garden becomes overgrown and needs a complete change.

Some terrarium plants are raised from seed but the majority are produced vegetatively from cuttings, offsets, or by other methods. Cuttings will need some help in their early stages to produce roots and become mature enough to plant. The main help that one can provide is a close atmosphere to reduce transpiration. If cuttings transpire too freely they simply shrivel up and die. The warm, close, damp conditions in the case will greatly assist rooting, as will firm and healthy plant material. Experiment with easier plants like tradescantias to begin with, inserting them in the potting mixture recommended for planting. The cuttings can go into small pots or be put into compost spread over the bottom of the container. Once rooted they can be used for decorative planting in a terrarium or bottle garden. Where several containers are kept permanently planted, it would be wise to have a spare used simply to propagate plants to be used for restocking as necessary.

CHAPTER 4

PLANNING A TERRARIUM

It is not usual to plan and plant one's own terrarium, as these decorative features are so often received as gifts with the plants already in place. The fortunate recipient has then simply to choose a suitable position for the unit and see to watering and general care. He or she will have missed the pleasure of creating something to their own particular taste.

There are three important aspects to consider when planning a terrarium – the choice of container, the choice and preparation of plants, and how the plants should be arranged – the design, if you like.

TYPES OF CONTAINER

These range from units capable of holding one to three plants to those large enough to resemble a traditional free-standing conservatory. You may find yourself with an old-fashioned bell glass, or a discarded fish tank – or one specially acquired with a plant arrangement in mind. The latter is probably best for a terrarium, being more spacious and offering considerably more scope for planting.

You will usually find a good selection of conventional terraria offered for sale in garden centres and department stores, some already planted, others simply glass cases awaiting your expertise to transform them into something interesting and decorative. Many smaller terraria are intended for wall decoration and are equipped to be attached to a picture hook or nail. Many of these can also be suspended, to become virtually miniature hanging baskets. Terraria intended for wall mounting are often provided with a built-in mirror that seems to give the unit greater depth, though this can be distracting if one glimpses unexpected reflections.

Little planning is needed when planting the smaller units as the amount of space inside limits the number of plants it can house. Even these should be small, unless one is thinking of letting the strands of trailing plants hang out of the container's open window. Some hexagonal-shaped units will have three open windows – ideal for trailing plants such as tradescantias or ivies. Almost all terraria will take at least 5 cm (2 in) of potting compost for planting, larger containers correspondingly more.

The real fun of terrarium planting comes from the larger units, as you can be so much more adventurous with your choice of plants and the overall design. But do avoid completely filling the container with plants, as your chosen plants must have space to develop new leaves. It is even more important to avoid plants growing in large pots, as the root ball will be difficult to fit into any but the largest terrarium.

The layout of medium-sized units is also largely governed by the space inside them. Taller plants generally have to be planted in the centre with smaller plants around or in the front of them. Some medium-sized units are like a grand Victorian style greenhouse with high sides and pitched roof. They are intended as a room centrepiece, and so are provided with decorative supporting legs or with a table to stand on. Like the more spacious fish tanks, they offer considerable scope for planting. There is space for paths and other garden features without pushing the plants so close together that they deteriorate. Whatever effects one has in mind, the plants' well-being *must* come first. Pebbles and other kinds of ornamentation can be used to allow extra space around plants, but draw the line at brightly coloured recumbent gnomes!

The bell glass is a relic of Victorian times and not easy to acquire, but I have two in my own collection, so they are still obtainable. These consist of a base with a glass dome sitting on top of it. Their main attractions are that they are different, and that the bell can be removed to make plant care easier, though problems can arise when plants become too large for the bell glass to fit comfortably over them.

My personal choice of plant container would be a fish tank, though it is rather stark and simple. This offers very good light for plants, as there are no bars or crosspieces as in a conventional terrarium. The plants look better and grow with that extra bit of sparkle. One of the major benefits of all terraria is that the plants can grow in their own microclimate and are free from damaging draughts. To create a similar environment in a fish tank one would have to provide it with a sheet of glass lid or buy a tank already provided with one.

DIY specialists might decide that, besides planting their own terrarium, they should acquire the components, solder them together and build their own. It is not difficult to assemble a terrarium following the instructions, provided you are a reasonably competent handyman. Buying the components and fitting them together will be more economical, though the end result might not be up to professional standard.

PLANT CHOICE AND PREPARATION

Advising on suitable plants for a terrarium is like the wisdom or otherwise of treading on thin ice – it might be all right, but it might be all

With a large terrarium, such as a fish tank, you can be adventurous when it comes to design. This planting scheme, which features cryptanthus, slopes down from back to front so that all plants can be seen to advantage.

wrong! One might fall through thin ice, and in ideal conditions a once-small plant could grow energetically and begin pushing the top off its terrarium! So advising on a choice of plants is done with considerable reservation. Once can only offer guidance based on past experience. And experience suggests that one should obviously select small plants for small terraria and preferably plants that are slow growing, or that will not be spoiled by some occasional careful pruning with scissors.

You will now find batches of plants at almost every garden centre and plant retailer's labelled as either 'tots' or 'plants suitable for bottle gardens' (Fig. 9). These may have been grown from seeds or cuttings and

Fig. 9 Foliage houseplants are sold as 'tots' for planting in glass units – when care in selection is necessary to avoid plants that are too vigorous. Always select plants of interesting shape and colour.

are produced in phenomenal numbers as, besides being suitable for bottle gardens, they are ideal cheap plants for anyone getting together a collection of indoor plants. Potting them into slightly larger pots at reasonable intervals – ideally when the existing pot is well filled with roots – and watching them prosper will provide the owner with a lot of pleasure.

One reason for 'tots' being ideal for a terrarium is that small pots naturally contain a small amount of potting compost and a small root ball is much easier to fit into the limited confines of the terrarium. But it cannot be over-emphasized that a small plant in a small pot is not the only criterion in making one's selection. For example, *Grevillea robusta*, the silk oak, an Australian tree with feathery foliage, might seem well suited as a slightly taller plant for a terrarium, but its prodigious rate of growth makes it one of the most unlikely candidates. Besides outgrowing their headroom, the more vigorous plants also take over all the available space in the terrarium, depriving the smaller plants of light and air, so they seldom prosper.

You could ask for advice from the staff on duty among the plants but, sad to say, it will not always be very satisfactory. You may be lucky, but the staff at most such premises consider a small plant in a small pot is a bottle garden plant and that is the end of it! The best advice for choosing suitable plants would be to go along with a list of the plants that are generally satisfactory. Such a list will be found on pp. 25–52.

Unlike plants in pots, many of the young plants raised from cuttings, such as ivies, can go straight into the terrarium from the seed tray in which they were rooted. It is often an advantage to use plantlets in this way, as their roots can be spread out and accommodated more easily, and the plant growth can be spaced to give better coverage than a similar number of cuttings restricted to a root ball.

Before removing plants from their pots for planting, they must be well watered by standing the pot in a bowl of water and holding it submerged until all the air bubbles have escaped. Having removed the plant from its pot, the next piece of advice is to remove a little of the compost on the surface of the root ball and dispose of it. This will dispose of any algae that may have formed or weed seeds that may be present. Occasionally a hard crust has formed on the surface of the soil and removing it will aerate the roots more efficiently.

If the layer of compost in the terrarium is only shallow you will need to tease away some of the compost at the bottom of the root ball, besides removing the hard crust on the surface of the root ball. Failure to do this will mean the root ball is only partially buried in the limited depth of compost in the container. Besides being less attractive, this will result in the small plant's roots drying out.

Besides ensuring that plants you buy are suitable for a terrarium, do make sure they contain no pests. Pick up your selected plants and invert them so you can inspect the undersides of their leaves for such marauders as white fly, aphids, scale insects and red spider mites. (More information on plant problems pp. 91–94). The confines of a terrarium or bottle garden are almost ideal breeding areas for most foliage problems, and so one would only have to introduce one or two pests when planting to put every plant in the container at risk. When planting, make sure that the compost is suitable and contains charcoal to prevent it becoming sour. (See also p. 72.)

DESIGN

The first element of terrarium design should be to use only quality plants in clean attractive containers. Dirty plants with brown and dying leaves in a container with grubby glass never look the part.

Having obtained some suitable compost and placed it in the container, having made sure it is moist you should then arrange your chosen plants

Larger units, such as this giant bottle, offer great scope in design and permit one to include some of the smaller flowering plants such as African violets (saintpaulias).

on an area equivalent to the inside area of the container to see how they look. If the arrangement meets with your approval, you can set about planting them. This is a far better approach than planting the container and then deciding the plants have to be rearranged. Never use very large or spreading plants in smaller units, as they will be difficult to fit in and equally difficult to arrange with any degree of balance and shape. Regardless of the size of the terrarium, all plants should have a little space around them, not be crowded together. In fact, the interior should have a rather sparse look to start with. With reasonable care the chosen plants will soon fill the spaces – in fact, as often as not they fill in too rapidly!

Whatever the size of the container, one must also endeavour to group together plants whose colouring is reasonably harmonious. Green foliage provides a good background for other plants and its colour will not be difficult to incorporate, but care is needed with stronger colours such as reds, pinks and yellows.

Larger terraria will offer much more scope and permit one to include some of the smaller flowering plants – *Saintpaulia ionantha* (African violet) in particular. The great advantage of a terrarium is that one can easily get a hand inside it to remove dead flowers and other debris, whereas the bottle presents much greater difficulty.

To achieve balance within the container it will be necessary to include some plants of reasonable height. Best of the slightly taller, more slender plants for this purpose are staked small-leaved ivies, *Dracaena* 'Red Edge', *D. sanderiana*, *Chamaedorea elegans* and *Dizygotheca elegantissima*. These are not just tallish plants but of slender habit, so demand less space in the upper part of the container.

One can do much more in the way of design and layout with a fish tank – depending on its size. You can provide an undulating surface with reasonable sized mounds of compost to improve the design, and larger units could include a gravel path running through the layout so that two complementary plantings could be included. It would also be possible to include small coloured stones in these units to provide variation in the design. If you have a woodland scene in mind, tree bark and even small tree branches could be used.

With terraria you could be constantly creating new designs by re-arranging the same plants or replanting when they become overgrown. Anyway, it should be a lot of fun and you will gain experience with every new design.

CHAPTER 5

BOTTLE GARDENS

CHOOSING THE BOTTLE

These can be many different shapes and sizes, with a little variation in colour to add flavour to the mixture. One could use an old-fashioned glass sweet jar to reasonably good effect for a few small plants. The traditional carboy with its protective wickerwork surround has become something of a rarity, and something to cherish if one becomes available. Its main advantage over today's containers is that the glass is clear, rather than green, which is much less attractive.

Not only are dark bottles less appealing, but when installed the plants do not thrive as well and look much less attractive. The principal advantage of modern bottle gardens is that they are much cheaper than their older counterparts. Today's bottles also come in several designs of differing sizes, some sold as 'onion bottles' on account of their squat onion-like appearance.

When purchasing an empty bottle for planting, first of all select one with reasonably clear glass, to encourage plant growth. The plants will be more clearly visible too. There seems little point in planting a miniature garden if it is obscured by a dark glass surround. To make planting easier, also opt for a container with a reasonably wide mouth through which plants and compost have somehow to find their way. Later in this chapter you will find information about simple tools for planting the more difficult bottles, but it is clearly much simpler if the bottle has a wide enough neck to get a hand in to arrange and plant the plants and look after them later.

PREPARATION

Handle all glass plant containers carefully. Bought containers must be properly packed (perhaps in an outer cardboard box) for the journey home. You may even need to buy a wrought iron stand for your bottle when it is finally planted and ready to be put on display. Such a stand will give the bottle a slight air of distinction – better than just standing it on the carpet.

Many bottles will have been manufactured abroad and have had a lengthy road journey before getting to their destination. So do not buy them in their outer cardboard containers without inspecting them to see that no damage has been done. When you get the bottle home, it will generally be coated with dust and possibly some of its protective straw covering. Your first task then ought to be to clean the glass thoroughly outside and in before giving any thought to planting.

Do not pour boiling water into the container: if the water is too hot the glass could easily break. Use tepid cleaning water with a little detergent added, and a soft cloth to clean the glass. Once clean it can be rinsed with cold water, then allowed to dry.

Part of your preparations will be shopping round for all the ingredients needed to make a success of your bottle garden planting. Simple planting and maintenance tools can easily be made, but compost, charcoal and gravel will have to be obtained on your shopping trip. It seems to make little difference whether you cork the bottle or not. A stoppered bottle will need little or no water, while the one left open may need an occasional dribble.

MATERIALS

When shopping for a bottle you could acquire the materials needed to prepare it for planting. Sufficient gravel will be needed to cover the bottom of the container about 5 cm (2 in) deep before compost is introduced. Clean, washed pea gravel is ideal for this purpose, but clean grit of similar size would also be suitable. Try to avoid using large chunks of stone, but in any event ensure that the drainage material is washed clean before it is introduced.

Perhaps the most important of all the materials to be placed in the container will be the growing compost, so choose the most suitable mixture available. A trowel or two of soil from the garden is *not* the answer! A properly prepared houseplant potting compost sold in a sealed bag will generally be best. But the quality of much of the potting compost offered for sale in this way leaves much to be desired, so it may be necessary to improve the compost when you tip it out of the bag for use. The mixture should have a nice feel to it when a handful is run through your fingers. If it feels stodgy or excessively wet, something has to be done to make it more agreeable to the plants to be set in this mixture. One way of doing this is to add some of the gravel or grit to the compost. Alternatively, if some Perlite is available, mix one third of it with two-thirds by volume of the compost to provide a better growing mixture. But it could well be that a little dry peat added to the wet compost will be sufficient to rectify matters. The important thing is not to put a wet soggy mess of compost in the bottle at the outset, or it will assuredly lead to problems later.

A fish tank can be fitted with a cover which incorporates a strip light to encourage plant growth. The plants also look more attractive when the light is on.

If planting is done with care there should be no need to include anything but plants in the bottle, but some of us cannot resist including some decoration in the way of cork bark or coloured stones with the plants. If you feel that such decorative materials are necessary, you need to obtain them while buying all the other ingredients. As often as not, any left-over gravel or grit will be fine for adding a colourful touch to the surface of the compost where there are larger gaps between the plants.

A small quantity of charcoal will also be essential. It is usually sold in small cartons or bags in garden shops. It is ready for use, so all one needs to do is mix it into the compost and introduce it into the container. Enough charcoal to fill an 8 cm (3 in) pot will be sufficient to prevent the compost in an average bottle from turning sour. If charcoal is not used, the compost will invariably become sour and unsightly green algae will

Fig. 10 Narrow-necked bottle gardens require a few simple tools to facilitate planting, all of which can be easily made from garden canes, twine/adhesive tape and the appropriate spoon, fork, etc.

form on the surface of the compost. This is not only ugly, but also detrimental to plant growth.

If you cannot buy a bottle with a neck wide enough to get a hand inside to plant the plants and perform the various essential chores, you will have to buy one with a narrow neck. You should then buy a few garden canes about 50 cm (20 in) long when getting the materials together. You can use these to make your own bottle garden tool kit. My kit consists of a spoon secured to a cane and used as a trowel, a table fork similarly attached used as a rake to aerate the compost, and a nail used as a spike to hold plants in position when planting and for getting out dead leaves. Another useful tool is a razor blade wedged into a cleft in the end of a cane and used as a pruner when plants get out of hand. As shown in Fig. 10 most of the tools can be fixed to the canes by twine.

DO-IT-YOURSELF

An ornamental Wardian case, built in the extravagant style of Victorian craftsmen, will be well beyond the scope of most people, but there is a great satisfaction in constructing your own terrarium.

Not many high street shops specialize in terraria, but you will find do-it-yourself kits for sale and perhaps demonstrated at many craft shows, flower shows and garden centres. A kit will contain the metal struts, glass, soldering materials and the like, but you will also need a heavy duty 75W soldering iron and a single-wheel tungsten carbide glass cutter.

The first thing to learn is that assembling your own terrarium is not a task to be rushed. Some of the operations take practice to get right, but start with something simple to avoid any costly mistakes, and progress to the more elaborate as your confidence and ability increase.

BUYING THE PLANTS

While shopping for your bottle and compost, also consider buying the plants that are to become its main feature. The best advice here is to say, don't overdo it. Select sufficient plants to make a pretty picture but at all costs avoid overcrowding. An average bottle takes about five plants, larger bottles perhaps seven, while a sweet jar can only take three at most.

Almost every garden shop worth its salt will have a selection of plants prominently labelled, 'Bottle garden plants'. But such a notice is no guarantee that the plants are not small rooted cuttings of kinds that could in time reach tree-like porportions totally unsuitable for the confines of a bottle garden. You can decide on their suitability by simply seeing which of the larger brothers of the 'bottle garden plants' still look neat and compact. Some of the plants may well be compact and slow growing, but this will be reflected in the asking price.

When selecting plants, remember that you will need at least one to give the arrangement a little height, perhaps two trailing or creeping plants and three of intermediate size. You can play about with the plants on the bench in the garden shop. See the assistant and ask for a small area to be cleared. Having bought the bottle and all the ingredients they should not object! Then make a circle in the gravel on the bench roughly the area of the interior of the bottle where the plants will be located and set out your plants in the most attractive fashion. There are two reasons for this – first, you only buy the number of plants you require, and secondly you know exactly where you are going to set the plants in the bottle. All being well, this should result in much quicker, more satisfactory planting. You perhaps need one more piece of equipment if the container has a narrow neck, and that is some sort of funnel to direct the various materials into the bottle. You can easily make a funnel from stiff brown paper shaped like an ice-cream cornet with the pointed end cut off to allow the compost to flow through evenly.

PLANTING

First to enter will be the gravel, which should be spread evenly across the bottom of the bottle (Fig. 11). Though not absolutely necessary, I find a thin piece of capillary matting cut to shape and placed on the surface of the gravel before the compost is introduced will ensure that compost does not gradually filter through into the gravel. Besides looking more pleasant the matting will keep the compost and gravel segregated and improve the drainage in the container. With luck you should be able to see if there is a build-up of water in the gravel – impossible if the gravel and compost become intermingled.

Then fill in with compost, directing it to the centre of the container so that the sides of the bottle remain as clean as possible. When filling, try not to put in more compost than necessary. The object is not to half fill the bottle with soil but simply to provide enough to cover the roots of the various plants once they have been placed in position. The compost can be spread evenly or, if preferred, can be given an undulating surface, but it makes little difference as the plants will soon cover the compost so little is seen. The compost should be moist but not saturated and the plants should be watered a little in advance. Never plant any that are dry at the root.

Keeping your planting plan in mind, make holes in the appropriate places with the spoon/trowel tool, then using this tool and the nail attachment to keep the plant on an even keel, lower it into position. The entire root ball of the little plant *must* be covered with compost, and this could well mean removing some of the soil from the base of the root ball. Either firm the plant into position with the spoon, or use a cotton reel on a cane to firm the soil around the plant. The importance of ensuring that the rootball of the plant is firmly embedded in the compost cannot be over-emphasized.

If the compost and the plants' roots were moist when planting, there should be no need for water, but if necessary a short length of hosepipe attached to the kitchen tap can be used to direct a trickle of water around the roots of the plants (Fig. 12). Use the same technique for any subsequent watering – never pour water into the container from a watering can with the spout perched on the lip of the container or you could wash all the compost from around the roots of the plants.

Ingredients for a bottle garden: a good quality houseplant compost; gravel to provide drainage; a selection of home-made, long-handled tools; and, of course, a suitable number of small plants.

AFTERCARE

Now stand the bottle in a light, but not sunny place and you should be able to sit back and watch the plants grow (Fig. 13). Given a reasonable temperature of around 15°C (59°), the plants in their warm, moist, draught-free bottle will generally grow very well – often too well, so that trimming shoots and even replanting may become necessary. Many plants, including ivies and *Ficus pumila* (creeping fig), will revel in these conditions and will need frequent attention from the razor-blade pruner.

Bottles filled with dead and dying plants can be a pain to look at but so can an untidy mass of plants with uncontrolled foliage. It pays to be brave and inspect the container regularly and remove any growth that seems to be outgrowing its welcome. Removing over-enthusiastic plants gives you the opportunity to plant afresh, perhaps with a different selection of plants, to maintain the interest. The same old bottle garden can become rather a bore and so, if only for this reason, one needs to ring the changes as often as practicable.

A typical collection of plants sold for bottle gardens, including ivies, selaginella, ferns and cryptanthus.

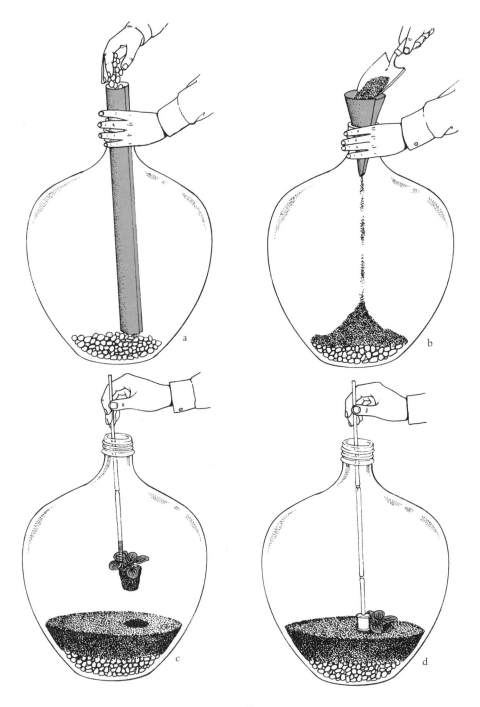

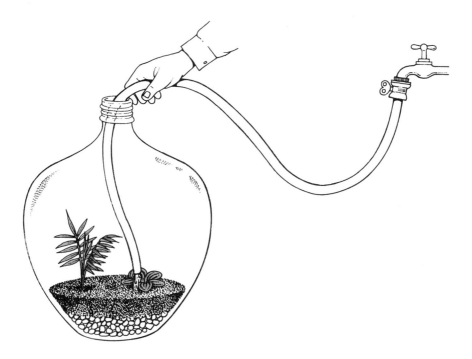

Fig. 11 *Opposite:* First clean the glass and then introduce gravel, charcoal and compost, using a cardboard funnel to direct materials into the desired position. Lower plants into prepared holes and firm gently into position using cottonreel tamper. Ensure reasonable space between plants.

Fig. 12 Bottle gardens need little water to succeed. Apply water carefully as a trickle through a hosepipe, the end of which should be almost touching the compost. Never water to excess.

REPLANTING

Change is one of the most important requirements in a display. So how often should the planting in a bottle be changed? If the planting and general conditions within the room are reasonably good, then an annual change of plants should be about right. Not all the plants will have out-grown their welcome in the space of twelve months, but some will in-evitably have grown more vigorously than others, so all the plants will have to be removed. Some of the less vigorous can be reintroduced to the

Fig. 13 The completed garden should contain taller, intermediate and lower-growing plants so that an attractive picture is formed. Dead and dying plant material should be removed at once, so avoiding future problems.

bottle when it is replanted, though almost all will need some tidying and trimming to reduce their bulk.

Larger plants, such as ferns, should be tidied up before being planted in flower pots of a size that will easily accommodate their roots plus a little additional compost to grow into.

Once plants have been removed the bottle should be thoroughly cleaned inside and out before fresh drainage material, compost and plants are introduced. Old compost, grit and other such materials should then be disposed of.

CHAPTER 6

PLANTING A TERRARIUM

One of the main differences between plants growing in pots and those in a terrarium is that in the latter everything is on view – the drainage material, the compost and very often the plants' roots. You pop the compost and the plant's roots into a pot and that is that, but you need to be more considerate with a glass container. One way of masking the otherwise exposed soil and roots would be to have a dish made that would fit perfectly into the bottom of the container to take the roots, soil and such-like.

The first step when planting any glass container is to ensure that the glass is clean inside and out. When cleaning make sure that the water is not boiling – tepid is much better. This is less important with terraria, however, than bottles, which are easily cracked when boiling water is used to clean them.

DRAINAGE MATERIALS

It is often impossible to provide drainage material in the bottom of smaller containers, as it would make it impossible to get enough compost in for adequate planting. But where containers allow for a reasonable depth of planting material it will help to begin preparation by first introducing a layer of drainage material, though not too much.

The drainage material fulfils two functions: first, when looking at the completed unit from the side it is more pleasing to see a contrasting layer of gravel than to look only at compost. It could even be an advantage to use coloured grit for drainage, simply to make the unit more attractive. Grit in a variety of colours and sizes is available from most good garden centres. Secondly, drainage material also prevents compost becoming soggy.

The compost that is spread over the drainage material will wash through and into the drainage material in time, making it less effective. To avoid this, spread a piece of thin capillary matting on the gravel. When the drainage material has been put into the container a sheet of paper can be placed over the surface and cut to roughly the right shape, then used as a guide to cut the matting to the correct size.

COMPOST FOR PLANTING

It is essential to get as much compost into the container as possible without producing an unsightly mountain of compost spilling out of the container and very difficult to handle artistically. Use good quality compost, adding grit to improve the drainage if necessary, or a material such as Perlite which will help to keep the compost open and aerated. Charcoal is another essential ingredient when planting. It is obtainable in crushed form from most plant shops. Work a good handful, perhaps a little more in larger units, into the compost to prevent it becoming sour. Unsightly green algae quickly forms on the surface of sour compost.

A small conventional terrarium offers little scope for design or imaginative planting as the space is so limited. It is simply a question of selecting three to five of the smallest plants available and grouping them in the most pleasing manner. A group of plants all of one kind can be as effective as anything in a smaller unit – *Hypoestes* 'Pink Splash', the polka dot plant, being a good example. Or it could be ivies, or tradescantias – even cacti if the container is to be stood in a reasonably light position.

PLANTS FOR A HANGING TERRARIUM

Small units acquire an extra dimension if trailing plants can be added to the planting. For trailers to be fully effective, either suspend the unit from an overhead anchorage or attach it to a wall. Any plant shop offering terraria will sell designs with one flat side intended for wall mounting, so they can be viewed from one side with some of the plants spilling out of its open windows.

Ceropegia woodii, which has the common names 'hearts entangled' and 'rosary vine', is a lovely plant for a suspended unit. In ideal conditions with a reasonable amount of compost its trails will in time reach to the floor. Its tiny tubular flowers are insignificant, but the thread-like stems bearing heart-shaped grey leaves are a constant source of interest. For something a little different one could use *Episcia dianthiflora*, a natural trailer that is easy to grow, and produces lovely white, snowflake flowers over a lengthy period during spring and summer. If you want a more generous show of summer flowers you can try *Campanula isophylla* with either white or blue flowers, the latter being much freer flowering.

Another favourite of mine for a smaller hanging container is *Streptocarpus saxorum*, which has succulent green foliage and the most delicate blue flowers you could ever wish to see – not wildly floriferous, but very pretty. A final personal choice among naturally pendulous plants would be *Begonia sutherlandii*, with pale green foliage and flowers of the brightest orange. The major drawback with this plant is its susceptibility to mildew. When the first powdery white spots are seen on the leaves, waste no time in applying a fungicide. Badly marked leaves should be removed. Where to buy these plants I've mentioned is a challenging question. Finding a source of supply will not be easy, but doing a bit of detective work to find some distinctly different plants is part of the fun of growing such things in bottles and terraria.

BUY GENUINE DWARF PLANTS
We often come across a gardener with limited space who has a conifer jungle that is becoming an embarrassment because its vigorous growth is totally unsuited to his small garden. You will find that the gardener bought the conifers believing they were dwarf plants that would remain compact. But what he really bought were conifers in small pots, plants that would mature into substantial trees. Remember the conifer man when shopping for terrarium plants and consider your purchases most carefully – don't simply buy plants because they are in small pots and look pretty. As already mentioned, one of the best checks when buying terrarium plants is to visit a plant shop that offers a good selection of houseplants, pick up the plants you fancy, then, before paying for them, just check the small ones in your hand against plants of the same kinds growing in larger pots around you to make sure you are not going to faced later with the same problem as the man who bought the conifers!

MINIATURE BROMELIADS
With the current popularity of air plants, the smaller bromeliads are enjoying a new lease of life. Good news for anyone interested in terraria. The smaller bromeliads, like tillandsias and cryptanthus, are as near perfect as you can get for planting in cabinets, as they take many years to develop to any significant size. And in the restricted quantity of compost in the terrarium they will never be likely to outgrow their welcome. Cryptanthus are classed as terrestrial bromeliads, as they grow on the floor of the jungle in their tropical American habitat, so they need to be low down in the terrarium. The tillandsias are tree dwellers and in a large unit can be attached to a small tree branch or a decorative piece of bark. Cryptanthus are familiarly known as earth stars as their rosettes of leaves look like the starfish one might see on a beach.

PLANTING TECHNIQUE

Having prepared the terrarium, fish tank, or other kind of container, it should already have its layer of drainage material, followed by compost carefully spread over the area and firmed with the fingers into the corners to ensure the plants good anchorage. It must be spotlessly clean, so do not make all the preparations and then start digging holes so dust flies around in all directions. The compost should never be dusty anyway but damp enough for moisture to be seen between your fingers when you squeeze a handful – not sodden, but nicely moistened.

As when planting a bottle garden, it is best to arrange the plants to be set in a terrarium or fish tank outside their container in roughly the area they will occupy when planted inside. Don't put plants in and take them out again to re-locate them, but arrange them outside the container, then plant them in exactly the right positions. Then there is no mess, no mutilation of leaves or other damage.

The worst kind of planting is where there is an inadequate amount of compost and the plants you have acquired are in excessively large pots. The limited amount of soil can then only accommodate half the root ball, so half the roots will be stranded in mid-air. Such plants will never look right and will certainly never thrive. If the root ball is too large, carefully tease away a good part of the lower section – don't just chop it off – to allow the root ball to be planted with a full covering of soil. This sort of treatment will not harm the plant as the soil is generally very peaty and plants in small pots bought for terraria will not have extensive roots anyway. Be sure to hold each plant firmly in position with a finger and then draw your fingers lightly over the soil surface to leave it with a natural appearance.

A GOOD MIX OF PLANTS

Terraria depend for the effect mainly on the texture, colour and arrangement of the plants within, rather than on any landscape effect. Unless the cabinet is very large there is little scope for creative landscaping anyway. A terrarium layout should be approached much as one would the planning and design of a flower arrangement. The right materials are essential for the latter, the correct height and balance of the various flowers and foliage and, perhaps most important of all, the right blend of colours.

THE RIGHT SIZES
You will need a good balance of tall, medium and low-growing plants. You need to see these in your mind's eye fitting harmoniously together when planted. You need some contrast in the style of plant you use – some with pointed leaves, some rounded, some feathery, and so on. The arrangement needs balance, probably with one taller plant to give some height at the back or in the centre, two, possibly three, intermediate plants, and low growing or trailing plants to complete the picture at the

Purpose-made hanging terraria are ideal units for trailing plants, of course. However, there are plenty of other kinds of plants can be planted in them, including ferns, as shown here.

front. After all, you are creating a kind of picture, something visually pleasing.

Besides visual pleasure though, we also have to think of the plants themselves. Unlike a painter or flower arranger, we have to ensure that our materials, the plants, will have a long and reasonably happy existence. One of the simplest yet most important ways of doing this is to allow them reasonable space to grow. Avoid the temptation to pack them in for instant effect. Far better to give them reasonable space and keep in mind the picture that will be presented to their admirers three, nine, perhaps twelve months hence. So there is another dimension to terrarium planting – creating for the future, just as one might when designing a garden.

COLOUR HARMONY

As with all flower arrangements and pretty pictures the need for colour harmony is paramount – no too hideously clashing hues. The terrarium planter is at a disadvantage compared with the flower arranger, as there is not such a wide choice of colours among plants as there is among the wide range of cut flowers. But perhaps with less to choose from there is less that can go wrong! However, a good plant shop will offer a wide range of plants. Have a chat with the person in charge, say what you are planning to do and ask if you can have a corner of a bench to set out some plants and get some idea how they are going to blend together when you get them home and start creating your own terrarium arrangement. The important thing is to *enjoy* it! If you get it wrong you can always do better next time!

SOME COLOUR SCHEMES

You could collect a number of plants with pale yellow/green colouring to be set off with blue flowered African violets. You could think of *Dracaena sanderiana* with whitish green striped leaves to provide the essential height in such a planting. It will attain a reasonable height in time, but will grow less slowly in a cabinet and will go on for a year or two without needing to be changed. At a lower level this greenish yellow arrangement could include *Peperomia magnoliaefolia*, which has a pleasing habit of growth and thick, succulent foliage that gradually develops into a neat mound. If the plants are very small when purchased, you could arrange two or three of them quite close together to obtain the right effect. Though robust in its rate of growth the golden tradescantia will creep over the surface of the compost with very pleasing effect, but do not allow it to get out of hand. To curb their invasive tendencies, regularly remove the growing tips of tradescantias. Alternatively, remove pieces of stem with two or three leaves for use as cuttings to make fresh plants. Whatever the chosen scheme always include at least one plant with green foliage to contrast with the brighter colours in the container.

The chosen colour scheme could well be red, though 'reddish' would be more accurate as there are not many really red coloured plants that are suitable – most tend to be deeper shades of pink. From our limited range of suitable taller plants the one that immediately comes to mind is *Dracaena* 'Red Edge', which has a pleasing dull reddish pink and pale green colouring. These plants are often offered for sale with three or four young plants growing close together in a small pot. These plants would not be suitable for planting in a confined space as they are. But water the plant and remove it from its pot and the individual plants can be teased apart to provide fine material for planting. Separating plants in this way will not harm them – their roots are generally limited and will easily tease apart in the small amount of peaty compost in which they are growing. At a lower level in the reddish arrangement you could use a *Begonia rex* with smaller leaves. (Avoid those with larger leaves, or the container could quickly become overgrown.) A *B. rex* could well start to develop larger leaves as the plants in the container grow. The simple remedy then is to remove them, complete with their leaf stalks.

Fittonias can cause problems when grown individually on a windowsill, but they are much less temperamental when grown in a warm, moist atmosphere. For a reddish effect one could use *Fittonia verschaffeltii*, a plant with beautifully veined leaves that will give constant pleasure. An alternative to saintpaulia in this sort of planting would be smaller plants of *Kalanchoe blossfeldiana*, which is available in a variety of colours. The commonly named polka dot plant, hypoestes, is available in varying shades of pink and has become one of the most popular of all foliage plants in recent years. It is a nice plant but is inclined to be invasive unless its more vigorous stems are removed occasionally. To enjoy all of these plants, do experiment to find the best ones for your purpose.

MINIATURE LANDSCAPES

Fish tanks are a different matter. They provide more room, so you can be creative and more imaginative in a landscaping rather than a flower arranging sense. But first you must find a fish tank. The easiest way is to go to your aquatics man and have a look at what he is offering for sale. You will find the range is much more varied than you imagined. Many of the units are much more elaborate than is necessary for our purpose, though you could consider tanks with internal lighting that will greatly

Some terraria have been designed for wall mounting and these units are ideal for trailing plants. Other plants can be used, though, such as asparagus and selaginella.

enhance your plants' appearance and improve their growth.

A fish tank, like other types of container, must be spotlessly clean and be provided with the essential drainage, soil and charcoal. But it will give you a larger planting area and better overall height, and planting will be much easier because of the improved accessibility. It is nigh on essential to include a path of coloured gravel to give it the landscaped garden look. Flowering plants like saintpaulias do specially well in tanks, as there is generally much better light for them to grow and they are more accessible for removing dead flowers and leaves. It is best to mound the soil towards the back of the tank and gradually slope it forwards, but leaving sufficient at the front for the plants that will finish off the arrangement. It is advisable to use rooted ivy cuttings and suchlike for the front rather than plants in pots which will be more difficult to set in place. When planting is complete to your satisfaction, add the finishing touch – the grit or gravel path at the front.

As with a flower arrangement, the plants in the tank ought to be taller at the back and gradually reduce in size towards the front. Avoid the temptation to fill every little space with plants. It is often much better to use reasonable sized pebbles, cork bark, or a small figure to fill gaps and give the arrangement more interest. As the plants begin to fill the gaps, the decorative features can be removed if necessary. Tanks will be the better for having a glass lid which reduces transpiration and almost eliminates the need for watering. It is essential to keep a high standard of hygiene and keep plants and glass as clean as possible.

CHAPTER 7

SPECIAL EFFECTS

With most forms of garden design and planting the plants should be the key features, but with terraria and bottle gardens one expects to have some licence when it comes to the materials used other than plants. Even the plants that are used might seem a little odd to a purist, but the whole subject of plants in cases is probably a bit of fun anyway!

LIGHTING

One sees specialist lighting used more and more for illuminating garden features during the hours of darkness, so there is surely justification for livening up glass cases indoors in a similar way. Instead of corking the top of a bottle garden it is not unusual to see a pedestal type lamp fitted into the neck of the bottle. In a darkish area this clearly benefits the plants in their glass sanctuary.

Many of the fish tanks displayed at the water garden store will have elaborate lids that incorporate an artificial light fitting. These should not be too powerful for plants, as they look best in subdued light. You can have special light tubes designed to improve the plants' performance, but plants are usually seen to best effect under an ordinary warm white tube.

Some forms of lighting, particularly spotlights, generate a lot of heat, so it is wise to use these only if they are a reasonable distance from the plants, otherwise the leaves could be scorched. Take special care where water and electricity are both present, obtaining professional advice to ensure no risk is involved.

AIR PLANTS

Today we see plants used in all sorts of ways to make them more appealing to potential purchasers. You see some kinds of cacti grafted on to other kinds, you see artificial flowers on pins being pushed into the tops of cacti to make it seem that they are in flower, and you see plants being fixed to shells with adhesive! Of all these strange tricks there is no doubt that the most successful is the last – air plants are now sold by almost every plant retailer in the land.

But what has this to do with plants in glass cases? Only that these air plants seem rather lost when stuck to a shell sitting on the kitchen windowsill. Wouldn't it be much nicer to group some together in a glass case – a fish tank, for example? It would be better for their appearance and they would grow better too because in a glass case they could be misted over and kept in a much more agreeable environment than their 'solitary confinement' on a windowsill.

You could perhaps contrive some form of plantscape with bits and pieces recalling these plants' natural tropical habitat in South America. You would need a different type of soil to grow these plants in a terrarium or fish tank, a mixture of peat and fresh sphagnum moss well worked in together. You could put this in the bottom of the container, then cover the surface with sphagnum moss, or bun moss if available. You could then put your tillandsias (air plants), cryptanthus (earth stars) and any other small bromeliads into this. To complete the effect introduce a few twigs or pieces of decorative bark.

A BROMELIAD TREE

Such a planting might tend to look flat and uninteresting so it becomes necessary to introduce something to give a little height. There are no taller growing forms of these miniature bromeliads, so you will have to provide some artificial means of creating height. The best way to do this is to find a firm but older piece of tree branch and fit it to some kind of base that can be hidden under the potting mixture in the bottom of the container. You can than attach a few of the smaller plants to its branches to form a miniature bromeliad tree that will give the terrarium far more interest than you would have believed possible.

Some of the best pieces of natural wood are to be found on the beach. Something washed with the tide and burnished by the sun is the sort of thing to look for. While beachcombing you might also collect an assortment of pebbles. Choose those of good colouring and of reasonable size, as one nice stone of good size is much better than a collection of smaller ones.

You can acquire all these items for nothing and they will give lots of pleasure when the time comes to be doing something a little different with the glass cabinet. Air plants will survive for long periods without water – in fact, it is often said they need no water whatever – but they will benefit from frequent misting over while in the glass cabinet. As with all plants, however, it is important not to overdo the watering in enclosed cases. Remember, there is nowhere for surplus water to go so it accumulates in the bottom of the container to the detriment of the plants.

A CACTUS GARDEN

You could also think of planting a cactus garden within the confines of a fish tank. These plants are tough and durable like bromeliads. This idea is perhaps less suitable for a more conventional upright terrarium, but a cactus garden in a table style terrarium with a good base area could look most effective.

Cacti and succulents will go for lengthy periods without water, but this does not mean that they prefer this sort of treatment. Far from it. If left dry and neglected during the spring and summer when they are more active in growth, they will quickly deteriorate. But during the winter months when the plants are dormant, they will go from early autumn until early spring with virtually no water and no feeding. But do water and occasionally feed them while actively growing in spring and summer. Never overdo the watering, of course, and grow all these plants in a special free-draining potting mixture. Water should run through the soil as it is poured on to the surface. A poorly drained mixture through which the flow of water is sluggish will never grow cacti successfully. As for feeding, you can now obtain special fertilizers for cacti. It goes without saying that you should heed the fertilizer manufacturer's advice set out on the label of the packet or bottle.

Having learned how to grow cacti, we now need to consider the best sort of arrangement for a glass container. First spread a little gravel or grit in the bottom of the container for drainage, then follow with some special free-draining cactus compost. As cacti and sand seem to go together it would seem a good idea then to cover the soil with sand. Alternatively, the plants can be planted first and the sand added last of all. You will then be spared the problem of having sand running into each hole you make to insert the plants. Sand varies in colour but the choice of colour should not be simply a matter of personal taste. It ought to be of a neutral colour so the plants provide the attraction and not the sand! Make sure, too, that you use washed horticultural sand, not the soft builders' sand which you might also find on sale at a garden centre.

There is such a fantastic range of suitable plants that it is well nigh impossible to make suggestions. People's taste is so different it seems best to recommend you visit a good plant shop or garden centre. There you will find an extensive range of cacti and succulents, many of them in the tiniest pots, ideal for the smaller terrarium. To obtain all your plants at the smallest stage of growth would be a mistake, as everything then looks lost. Much better to have a selection of varieties of different sizes. Consider an opuntia (prickly pear) or two, perhaps a euphorbia or cereus, to provide the arrangement with some height. No cactus arrangement would be complete without mammillarias, of which there is an extensive range of named varieties, many almost guaranteed to flower after their first watering in spring following their winter rest. Another genus of plant similar in shape to the mammillarias is the rebutias. If you are unable to make these flower there really is something amiss!

Cacti can look rather sparse on their own and might need a little help to look effective. You could put extra plants in the container, but crowding these plants together looks most unnatural. But you could possibly have a desert scene painted as a backcloth to fit the back of the fish tank type of container so that when viewed from the front the display will appear to have much greater depth.

Once planted, cactus arrangements must be stood in the lightest possible position, though at the same time make sure that the plants are not exposed to excessively hot sun. The sun's rays can be damaging when magnified by the glass. Most cacti are not bothered by fluctuating temperatures, but they do need frost protection in winter.

A JAPANESE GARDEN

Yet another different approach could be a cabinet offering a Japanese effect – one of those tranquil gardens with very few plants, one or two nice accessories and light-coloured sand. Again it will be much easier to make a Japanese style garden in a fish tank container as it provides a larger planting area. Space is of the essence with this style of garden. For the few plants you would need something like a parlour palm, *Chamaedorea elegans*, which could simulate bamboo, a peperomia as a miniature shrub with, say, the variegated trails of 'Sonny' (a nice variegated *Ficus pumila*) creeping over a flat stone.

All the stones in a proper Japanese garden have a meaning and their placement is significant, but for a living-room arrangement you would have to select two or three stones of pleasing appearance and locate them wherever they looked best. Use attractive grit in the bottom of the container, then a good houseplant potting mixture. When the plants are in position you would then cover the surface of the soil with light-coloured sand. The surface of the sand can then be carefully raked with a table fork to create a nice line pattern. Blocks of line patterns going in different directions can look very effective, and certainly different.

Finally, why not get hold of one of the currently fashionable indoor bonsai trees? Most of these are too large for an average terrarium, but you occasionally come across suitable smaller bonsai that could provide the perfect special plant. Most bonsai, like their full-sized counterparts, are outdoor plants – an oak or a pine, however small, will not be happy for long indoors, so look out for a species used to a warmer climate – perhaps a miniature gnarled, windswept olive tree. Such a plant may not be pretty in itself, but is ideal for creating the typically Japanese effect of serenity and age.

You could perhaps be excused for including a dish of water in a Japanese garden to represent the tranquil garden pool. With luck you might even get some reflections in the water by way of a bonus! Running water seems out of the question, but there are doubtless some people who could even overcome this problem.

OTHER TYPES OF GARDEN

All kinds of garden could be considered for miniaturizing. Woodland gardens always appeal to me and it might just be possible to create such a garden in miniature by using fallen leaves, say, to give the immediate feeling of a woodland – perhaps beech leaves reduced in size with scissors so that they are in proportion to whatever else is used. Obtaining small mounds of bun moss from the woods should pose no problem unless you live in a city.

You only have to consider what can be done and you are on your way. You can have a woodland path using brown loam instead of dark potting soil to provide a woodland feel. If it is firmed down and goes off at a wiggle you will be halfway towards the woodland. Plants for the floor of the wood could include the bun moss, selaginella in variety, small ferns and some of the many sorts of ivy available. What could be more suitable for a woodland than that?

What about trees? You have just got to have a clump of trees. My suggestion is that you go to your plant shop and buy a couple of pots of *Chamaedorea elegans* (also named *Neanthe bella*) and have a good look at them before you buy. Select those that have several young plants in a clump in the centre of the pot. Then when you get home you can water the soil, remove the plants from the pot and tease them apart and pot each separately in a small pot. They will seem rather thin and wispy, but will be fine if allowed to settle for a few weeks to develop good root systems. After all this work you can use your young parlour palms to create a copse or small clump of trees in your woodland scene. You might even be excused for including a miniature gnome in your woodland garden, sitting on his toadstool, spots and all!

Rock gardens, formal bedding and water gardens would seem to be out of the question for a garden in a terrarium, but you will see from the foregoing that, on the contrary, there are plenty of possibilities once you put your mind to it.

WINDOW GARDENS

In some parts of the world the terrarium has taken on a new dimension, becoming part of the homestead at the time the building is constructed. A sort of double glazing is provided with an outer and inner glass wall, set a considerable distance apart. In a deep window the frame forms the sides of the plant case, the sill forms the floor and the inner and outer panes complete the terrarium effect. The inside glass can be fitted so that it will slide or lift to facilitate planting and maintenance.

You have as much a miniature greenhouse as a terrarium. The advantages of such an enclosed area are considerable – particularly that you can include much taller and bolder plants. You could even consider housing a small orchid collection, planted in appropriate compost with moss and an old tree branch to create the right sort of setting. With a little thought, the sides of the window could be made from some waterproof material so the plants can be attached to tree branches and grown on the sides of the window, making the display much more appealing.

Given the height and greater space of such a window enclosure one could also grow some of the more exotic pendulous members of the *Gesneriaceae*. Columneas with their brilliant orange-coloured flowers would make almost perfect inhabitants. Some of the more exotic marantas, such as *M. makoyana*, and calatheas, such as *C. picturata*, would provide a wealth of foliage colouring to brighten virtually every day of the year. Be careful not to select a southerly aspect for a window terrarium, as bright summer sun would have a disastrous effect on almost all the plants in such a miniature hothouse. If the window has to be on the sunny side, then some sort of awning would have to be fitted to protect the plants.

CHAPTER 8

CARE AND MAINTENANCE

BUY WELL CARED FOR PLANTS

Success or failure with growing plants in a terrarium or bottle garden depends to a large degree on the kind of plants you initially purchased. Quality plants suitable for the job can have more influence than all the tender loving care the plants may subsequently enjoy. So my first piece of advice may seem unconnected with tending plants – before anything else, pay special attention to the plants you are buying, the place where you are buying them, the conditions they are in, and, not least, the sort of person in charge of retailing the plants.

There was a time when plants were bought from an experienced gardener or nurseryman, but you can now purchase them from almost any sort of retailer – a local garage selling petrol or even a newsagent. They may cost less at such outlets, but the plants will almost invariably be inferior, some more dead than alive after being exposed to the elements, apparently forgotten on the pavement outside the retail premises. Of course, you could be lucky and buy your plants the day they arrive from the grower. This is really the only way when buying from an inexperienced person as plants rapidly deteriorate in their hands.

Many of the plants are reasonably tolerant, but others are more temperamental and certainly vulnerable to unexpected cold periods. All the plants being sold will have come from agreeable, often heated premises, so they will suffer a severe shock when inconsiderately handled or stood in some cold inhospitable spot. For tender plants there is nowhere quite like a warm greenhouse cared for by an understanding person, so consider the feel of the premises when you go shopping for your terrarium plants. It should feel moist and warm and be ventilated on warmer days throughout the year.

Besides these points you ought to see one or two people inside the greenhouse watering, cleaning and generally taking an interest in their charge – the sort of person you can sneak up to and ask for advice on selected plants, knowing that you will get correct information. It is also essential to inspect plants for pests when buying them. No point in buying plants *and* pests, diseases or other troubles that might have set up home on them. With pests, prevention is better than cure, and best of all is not to acquire them in the first place!

CLEAN GLASS AND GRAVEL

It will greatly reduce your problems if everything you put into your terrarium or bottle garden is meticulously clean. The container should be washed inside and out, the gravel ought to be clean – washed in running water if necessary – and the compost should be clean and pest free, not dug up from the garden for the job. The amounts of materials needed are very small, but it is wise to obtain the best available.

The grower of plants or the person in charge at the retail shop is often confronted by a customer with a plastic bag in his or her hand and a worried expression that all too clearly indicates that there is some decomposing plant material in the bag. Sometimes the contents are the unrecognizable remains of the precious plants that were sold in perfect conditions only a few weeks before – plants for a terrarium perhaps! The retailer will stroke his chin considerably as he listens to the tale of woe – generally without uttering a word, so that he can get the full picture and put his finger on the reason for the disaster.

Having listened, he might then take the collection of debris in his hand and gently squeeze the compost around the roots of the plant. Water flows fairly freely between his fingers. He really has to say little more except that the plants have been drowned following over-zealous use of the watering can. More plants die from too much water than ever do from not getting enough. True of plants growing in pots, it is doubly true of plants in bottles and terraria. Plants have a chance in a pot, as the drainage holes in the bottom allow surplus water to drain away, but in a container with a sealed base there is nowhere for surplus water to go. The compost just becomes ever wetter, the plants' roots rot and die and their leaves then follow suit.

WATERING

When watering your plants in their container be sure that they really need some. Slightly dry soil will benefit most plants as they will then have to forage for moisture and consequently build up a more vigorous root system. Terraria with open windows will need more water than those that are completely closed, but bottle gardens will need only minimal watering.

Water terraria with a small watering can fitted with a long spout. Pour just a little water on to the compost initially and let it penetrate the surface of the soil before giving any more. The compost takes a little time to absorb water, so if a lot is poured on to it at once you will find that most of it will run to the sides of the container and over the lip on to the carpet below!

When watering plants in a bottle garden it is best to use a short length of hosepipe attached to a tap with the other end almost touching the compost in the container, so that water can be gently trickled around the plants. If water is poured from the mouth of the bottle it will travel with too much force and tend to wash the compost away from the plants' roots. It is advisable to use tepid water rather cold for terraria and bottles – remembering that tepid means with the chill off, *not* boiling water from the kettle! Bear in mind when you think of watering that plants are better a little on the dry side rather than too wet. Dry conditions can be remedied, but very wet conditions, particularly in bottles, can be death to the occupants.

You can now purchase simple inexpensive pieces of equipment to take the guesswork out of watering. You can read off the dial whether the compost is dry, wet, or in the right condition.

FEEDING

To feed or not to feed is a constant question with plants in bottle gardens, and to some extent in terraria. Unless plants in bottles are looking dis-coloured it should not be necessary to feed them. Feeding plants gener-ally stimulates more vigorous growth, and so your planting could well become overgrown.

You may well have temporary plants in terraria to provide extra colour. If they are still in their pots it will clearly be helpful to give them an occasional weak feed to keep them in good condition. Larger con-tainers, where a little additional growth will not be an embarrassment, can also be fed with weak fertilizer. You may also need to feed plants spilling out of the windows of containers and trailing downwards, but never simply feed plants for the sake of it – nor at set intervals regardless of whether they need it or not.

GOOD HYGIENE

A high standard of hygiene is vital for bottles and terraria. Never neglect any suspect material, dead or diseased as fungus infections like botrytis thrive on decaying matter. Dead leaves do nothing for plants, so remove them and give other plants in the container a better chance to prosper. When regularly cleaning up, it pays to check the plants for pests and deal with these promptly.

With bottle gardens particularly, a frequent difficulty is not poor growth but overactive growth – growth which, if plants are not chosen with care, can fill the container so that the less vigorous plants have the life choked out of them. Always be ready to wield the razor blade pruner to curb the plants that seem to be getting too vigorous for their surroundings.

Cleaning away and trimming discoloured leaves and branches in a terrarium presents few problems, as everything is easily accessible with a pair of sharp-pointed scissors. But a narrow-necked bottle into which one cannot get one's hand presents more difficulties. Tools for working inside the bottle have been described earlier (see p. 63). All are simple to make and can be used like chopsticks to cut away dead growth and to fish out the pieces after pruning. It is vital to remove the dead pieces and not leave them lying in the bottom of the bottle.

It will also be beneficial to break up the surface of the compost in the container occasionally with a pointed stick or plant cane. It is like hoeing the garden as it helps to aerate the soil and make it more open and attractive. Any algae that have formed on the surface of the soil should be carefully removed and not just broken up so they grow afresh.

THE OVERGROWN CONTAINER

There will come a time when the over-vigorous plants in a terrarium or bottle garden call for some action. They cannot be expected to go on for ever in such a confined space. Some plants will completely suffocate their neighbours in a case or bottle, one of these being the velvet nettle, *Gynura sarmentosa*. This is a lovely plant when seen growing on a windowsill with the rays of the sun catching the bright purple foliage, but it is a very unwise choice for a confined space. It is not unusual for it to produce stems more than 1.8 m (6 ft) long in a bottle and for the top of the plant to be outside the bottle considering where to go next. Similarly with badly chosen ferns. *Nephrolepsis exaltata* may look ideal when growing in a small pot, but it is not a good choice for any sort of enclosed case or bottle. You need have only one leaf go rotten in a bottle garden for all the plants in the container to develop botrytis, a dreadful fungus disease that will quickly spread until all the plants become a mushy mess of rotting foliage.

But it is not all gloom and doom. Serious problems only arise as a result of indifferent care and attention, perhaps because one is reluctant to dismantle a display that has been much admired over several months. Dismantling a terrarium presents little difficulty as one can get both hands inside the container to disentangle the plants and remove them individually. Some terraria and fish tanks have lids that can be lifted off to facilitate maintenance. It is then a simple matter to remove overgrown plants by putting one's hands into the container to grasp the lower parts of the plants and lift them out of the container, complete with compost. Discard the really poor plants as it is seldom worth trying to revive them. Larger plants in better condition can be potted individually and used about the house as pot plants.

Overgrown plants in a bottle are a much more serious problem. This is one good reason for not allowing plants to become too overgrown before they are controlled. Bottles with larger openings through which one can get a hand can be dismantled by using a sharp short-handled knife to cut around the roots of the plant. It can then be removed with a section of root that will come through the neck of the bottle without much difficulty. For a narrow-necked bottle you will have to attach a short-handled knife to a stout garden cane and use this to reduce the size of the rootball before removing it. Inevitably overgrown plants taken from a narrow-necked bottle will have to be mutilated to get them through the narrow opening. Plants from this type of bottle will have to be thoroughly cleaned and broken leaves and stems cut away before they are potted for future use. Surely the moral here is to avoid using narrow-necked bottles wherever possible!

CHAPTER 9

PESTS AND DISEASES

'Prevention is better than cure' is a phrase often applied to pests on plants, but it is doubly important when the plants are grouped in the narrow confines of a terrarium or bottle garden.

PREVENTION

How to prevent pests getting on one's plants when the atmosphere is filled with them may seem rather puzzling. I consider the most important measure is not to introduce pests to one's collection by 'buying' them from the retailer on plants purchased from him. So don't pick them up and take them to the till. It takes little effort to select plants that look clean and fresh and then to inspect the growing points of ivies for aphids, the undersides of plants in general for whitefly, red spider mites, scale insects and even mealy bug. If you are very bold you might go so far as to invert the pot and remove the plant so you can inspect its roots for vine weevil larvae. These troublesome pests can have a devastating effect on plants as they gnaw away at their roots.

Also by way of prevention it will do no harm on getting new plants home to treat them with a general insecticide, or apply a systemic insecticide that will deter pests for a longer period.

Fortunately, young plants bought for terraria are generally free of problems, with perhaps the exception of aphids which prefer soft green tissue to older, tougher parts of plants. Young begonia plants may also show the signs of powdery white patches on the upper surfaces of leaves which indicate that mildew is present. Treat all newly acquired plants with a fungicide too, if either mildew or botrytis is suspected.

TROUBLESOME PESTS

APHIDS

These embrace a wide variety of sap-sucking insects that multiply at an alarming rate in conditions that are agreeable to them. Young foliage that has been attacked may not at first sight appear to have suffered any damage, but as leaves of such plants as *Chlorophytum capense* (spider plant) mature it may be found that they have unsightly spots and blotches. This occurs as a result of aphid attack when their leaves were just beginning to develop.

If there are only a few aphids on the tips of young shoots the simple remedy is to run the shoot between your finger and thumb to wipe out the pests. Greater numbers of pests can be treated with one of the many available insecticides or a systemic insecticide can be watered on the compost so that it is working for you all the time. Some systemic insecticides are available in pellet or tablet form and have only to be pushed into the compost around the roots to have effect for several weeks. Some of them also incorporate a fertilizer.

MEALY BUGS

This is a pest that makes no attempt at concealment as it sets up home between the stems of plants, among the flowers or in almost unreachable places between the spines on cacti. Mature bugs are quite large and look rather like woodlice that seem to have been treated to a liberal coating of flour, hence their name of mealy bug. Killing the adults with a proprietary insecticide is not too difficult provided you can make make direct contact. Disposing of the babies is different though, as the parents wrap their offspring in a waxy cotton-wool-like substance that is difficult to penetrate with insecticide.

The 'cotton wool' is a sure sign that these bugs are present, as is the sooty mould deposit left on leaves beneath where the bugs are active. (Sooty mould is a fungus that grows on the excreta of these bugs and is very unsightly when seen in quantity on larger plants.) The easy way to eradicate these pests is to clean them from the plant with gentle force using an old toothbrush soaked in methylated spirit or insecticide. The good news is that these pests are not normally found on young plants but seem to prefer older plants with twisting stems, such as stephanotis which provide reasonably safe breeding areas.

But bugs could also be found on young cactus plants, so inspect these carefully when buying them. An infestation of bugs on a collection of cacti can be very troublesome as the many spines make them difficult to reach. You should be aware when checking cacti that some of the plants have a natural downiness around their spines which can easily be mistaken for mealy bugs.

ROOT MEALY BUGS

As its name implies this pest attacks the roots of plants. It is less common and less troublesome than the ordinary mealy bug. To detect it you have to remove the plant from its pot and look for creatures of similar appearance to their aerial brothers, but possibly a little smaller. There will also be signs of a powdery white deposit on the inside of the pot and around the roots. The best deterrent is a thorough drenching of the roots with an appropriate insecticide. Again, they are specially fond of cacti, but are not likely to be seen on young plants.

RED SPIDER MITES

These are perhaps the most destructive pests of all on houseplants. In warm, dry conditions they can create havoc with many of our indoor plants – and the confines of a terrarium are frequently hot and dry, so be warned. These mites are very small and barely detectable to the naked eye. To add to the problem they tend to be flesh coloured rather than red. Green leaves that turn a pale shade of brown are an indication that the mites are in residence, so avoid any such plants. They are particularly fond of ivies and will be seen on the undersides of leaves to begin with. As the infestation develops they spin webs between the main stem and leaf stalks, by which time you should consider discarding the plant as a lost cause.

Infected plants should be treated thoroughly immediately you notice the symptoms. You can spray the foliage, but younger plants are more effectively treated by plunging the pot in a container of insecticide. Wear rubber gloves.

SCALE INSECTS

These pests particularly favour certain kinds of plant, citrus and ficus being two of them, and are mostly found on mature rather than very young plants. But you need to be able to recognize these insects that cling like limpets to the undersides of leaves and the stems of numerous plants, sucking the life out of them. Older scales are dark brown, though young ones are flesh coloured. The best treatment is to don rubber gloves and use a sponge soaked in malathion solution to forcibly clean the pests from the plant. After this a careful watch and clean over with a damp sponge should eradicate any remaining scales.

WHITEFLY

These multiply at an alarming rate and are generally found on the under-sides of plant leaves. Easily detectable, they will fly away from the plant if the leaves are gently brushed. The plants most troubled by these pests are probably poinsettias and fuchsias, neither of which could be considered for a terrarium. A few individuals can be rubbed off with your fingers, but larger numbers should be sprayed with a recommended insecticide, repeating the treatment several times at four-day intervals.

DISEASES

Mildew is the most common disease and appears as a white powdery deposit on the upper surfaces of leaves of plants such as begonias. Inspect carefully when purchasing. **Botrytis** is less often encountered, but can be very troublesome in damp, airless places like terraria, so take care. Botrytis particularly favours dead and dying foliage and can cause considerable damage. So keep everything spotlessly clean. Both diseases can be treated with a fungicide, but good hygiene is the best deterrent.

INDEX